Spirit of Courage

Spirit of Courage

Letting go of Abandonment, Shame and Hurt

Tracie Saunders

Spirit of Courage: Letting go of Abandonment, Shame and Hurt
Copyright © 2013 by Dr. Tracie Saunders
All rights reserved.

Published by:
Professional Woman Publishing, LLC
www.pwnbooks.com

ISBN: 978-0-9894428-9-3

Printed in the United States of America

Contents

Introduction		i
1	Why God Why?	1
2	The Truth Shall Set You Free	13
3	The Ups and Downs of Abundant Living	27
4	Taking Care and Care Taking	39
5	Waging War	49
6	Courage in the Face of Friendly Rejection	63
7	Worship instead of Worry	73
8	Desperate Prayer	85
9	Universal Precautions and Hospitality	93
10	Keep Moving Forward	101
11	It Takes Courage to go to China	115
12	It Takes Courage To Be In Heaven....Now	121
13	Courage to be the Voice of Oppressed Women	129
About the Author		133

Dedication

This book is dedicated to all of the hurting women of the world. I pray God that this book will reveal the generous promise of healing (mind, body, soul, and spirit) that Christ offers the daughters of God and they will have the courage to receive it.

Introduction

Be on your guard; stand firm in the faith; be courageous; be strong. Do everything in love.

—1 Cor 16:13-14

The card says that Tracie means courageous. This is true. I have always been courageous. I've always felt like there is something protecting me from danger. My whole existence takes courage. For a black woman in the United States of America, to live a successful life takes courage. To be a wife takes courage to trust another fallible human being. To do what it takes to get into medical school takes courage. To practice medicine takes courage. I could credit my courage to my mother, a strong black woman who raised me to be independent and responsible for myself and to always speak up for what is right. I could credit my academic courage to Spelman College. I was amazed at all of the awesome, intelligent, professional Black people I met in Atlanta. I never could get that insight in Suffolk County, Long Island, New York. But the truth of the matter is that my courage comes from the almighty God.

The spirit of courage comes from God. God breathes courage into us just like God breathed life into us. An interesting thing about the spirit of courage is that you need to have it before you need it. It already has to be a part of your being before you need it. Jesus breathed on the disciples to give them courage to do the mission. There is this children's video program called "Bibleman" that teaches children about scripture. I watched it with my kids. Bibleman is a strong, kind, compassionate bible quoting superhero. The first scripture my kids memorized, not because they had to but because they heard it so much is, "no weapon formed against you shall prosper." (Isaiah 54:17) This scripture is the foundation of the spirit of courage. This is the same spirit that gave the shepherd boy, David, courage to kill bears, lions, and a giant.

It took courage for David to be a shepherd boy and to be a king. It takes courage for us to be all that God created you and me to be too. It takes courage to celebrate Thanksgiving everyday and not because it is an American holiday that has its roots in marginalizing other people.

It takes courage to tell a surgeon that you won't provide anesthesia for his patient because the patient is not properly prepared.

It takes courage to speak up at faculty meetings.

It takes courage to preach the Gospel of Jesus.

It takes courage to get married just for love.

It takes courage to get pregnant while an anesthesiology resident.

It takes courage to tell your boss you answered the call to the Gospel ministry.

It takes courage to tell your mother that she is wrong. (At least it did when I was a child.)

INTRODUCTION

It takes courage to ask your boss if you could work part-time in order to go to seminary.

It takes courage to forgive. Sometimes we humanize forgiveness too much and relinquish our responsibility to God. We say stuff like, "you can't do it but God can," or "forgiveness is a decision not a feeling." The truth is we need divine courage to truly forgive and then we get divine peace.

The spirit of courage is the opposite of the spirit of fear. The spirit of courage is what God has given us because of our faith in Christ. It consists of power, love, and a sound mind.

The spirit of courage is amazing, wonderful, and powerful. But it doesn't feel good. For us humans, it doesn't feel good. In the gut, it feels yucky. The throat has a lump in it. The heart is pounding. It feels horrible, physically. It is enough to make you want to retire to your bed forever. But you don't. To make you give up, but you can't. The spirit of courage makes you continue the path, this mission, and the purpose that physically makes you sick.

The spirit of courage stems from profound faith in something or someone. The more powerful the source, the more powerful the spirit of courage. Faith in logic, reason, medicine, science, etc. is powerful and makes sense. The secular world relies on these disciplines. But my spirit of courage, stems from the omniscient, all-powerful God.

The spirit of courage has no gender. Just like God has no gender. God is a spirit, neither male or female. God does not have a penis or testicles. However, there is a scripture that says that God is many breasted! Seriously, this book is about the spirit of courage that originates from the almighty God.

ONE

Why God Why?

About three in the afternoon Jesus cried out in a loud voice, "Eli, Eli, lema sabachthani?" which means "My God, my God, why have you forsaken me?"

—MATTHEW 27:45-47, MARK 15:34

*See, I have refined you, though not as silver;
I have tested you in the furnace of affliction.*

—ISAIAH 48:10

Growing up we would ask our parents -Why? And they would bark back, "Because I said so!" I even had courage as a child to challenge my parents for logic and reason at the risk of my life, or so I thought. I was always getting in trouble with my mother in particular because I came out and said whatever I thought, even if it was criticizing adults. In those days, children were "to be seen and not heard." In general, adult reasoning was on a need to know basis and children did not need to know. Children by definition could not have any wisdom because they were too young. The rule was that adults were always wiser than children. Of course we know this nonsense to be false. Today things are markedly different. In fact, parents may have gone too far in the other direction. Now the youngest of children debate with their parents over things such as sitting in a car seat, going to bed, public behavior, going to Sunday School, etc. Of course it is important for children to be seen and heard.

When it comes to God, our parent in heaven, we are able to be seen and heard by God because of Jesus. God is holy and cannot be in the presence of the un-holy or the sinful. If it were not for Jesus, humans would not be able to have a direct relationship with God. No effective prayer, no comfort, no deliverance, souls not saved from eternal damnation without Christ. This is why the passion story is so important. It is a brutal reminder of the crucifixion cross that Jesus willingly suffered for us.

Crucifixion was the Roman's favorite death sentence for guilty criminals of the state. Those condemned to crucifixion carried their own cross. After Jesus suffered the most horrific flogging, while he was bleeding and dying from his wounds, he had to carry his cross to atone for our sins. We're guilty, Jesus was innocent. Jesus could have called on 10,000 angels to rescue him from the cross but he didn't. Jesus bore the sins of the world, yours and mine so that we could have the opportunity to be seen by God. To be heard by God. To be healed by God. To be delivered by God. To be filled with the Holy Spirit. Hallelujah, praise the Lord.

While hanging on the cross, Jesus cried out, "My god, my god, why have thou forsaken me." In other words, "The god of me, the god of me, why have you left me!" These final words on the cross show humanity of Jesus. Jesus was fully human and fully divine walking on earth. Jesus suffered six hours before he made that last cry. Not only do we thank Jesus for dying for our sins so that we could have eternal life but we also thank him for showing us what to do when we can't take it anymore.

My God, my God, why have you left me behind. Jesus is communicating with God. This is prayer. Thank God for Jesus that he died on the cross so I'm able to pray. I know I'm seen and heard by God. What about you? Do you believe that Jesus died on the cross to save you from your sins? Are you seen and heard by God?

Jesus' cry out to God is not pretty or eloquent. But this shout out to God is effective prayer. This has to be the first prayer of an intercessory prayer warrior. The most important part of the prayer is "m**y** God." Acknowledging who God is and claiming God as one's personal possession is critical. God is mine. When I asked my 19 year old daughter, Amanda, "who does God belong to?" she answered, "whoever wants him." Yes, that's the whole point. God is mine, and God can be yours too. But don't think I'm crazy for possessing God for myself; for having affirming and abiding trust in God. Our merciful god heard this prayer and ended the suffering immediately. Instead of cursing God, Jesus latched on and claimed the Father as his God. This is what we are suppose to do, latch on to God. Always remember who God is to you personally. We have to endeavor to maintain a close, intimate, and personal relationship with God because we will need it when all hell breaks loose. Like when you find out that your precious child is in trouble and you can't fix it.

We went to Monterey, California for a convention, me and my husband. The pacific coast is beautiful. The driving is a little scary with the cliffs and turns, but we managed. While I was in a lecture, my phone rang and it was a call from my son's high school but it dropped. Then I text my 14 year old son, "Are you ok?" He answered, "No they are accusing me of something I didn't do." He was being questioned by the assistant principal and the police were involved. He was immediately suspended from school and my husband and I were three thousand miles away. It took four months and four days for him to be vindicated and reinstated back into school. From May 3 until September 7 my son was suspended from school.

WHY GOD WHY?

Today is September 7 and I probably should be happier, but I am not. I honestly don't know what I am. For four months and four days I have been scared for my son. But, I believed God. All along, I was waiting for God to fix everything. But the longer it took, the more mad I got. I'm probably being bad but truthfully, I don't think it had to be so bad for so long for me. I am God's favorite and so is my son. It could have been worse. Criminal charges could have been made and he could have been arrested and detained. Don't get me wrong God, I am truly grateful for your faithfulness to us, but it was horrible for me. I think I took it harder than anybody. My husband and my son were "cool" all along. Not me. I'm crying now writing about it. Is this what life is going to be about with my kids as they grow older? Am I going to be able to handle it. I know scripture says, "God doesn't give us more than we can handle." But this time he got way too close for me.

Every time I see a police car the feeling of fear comes over me. Every time I rounded the corner to my house I was looking for a police car. Every time the door bell rang I wondered if it was the police coming to arrest my son. I was worried about my son's mental status. So, I stayed as close to him as I could. We were always together. I tried to do everything I could to keep his spirit uplifted. I made sure that we remained as normal as possible. I did such a good job that no one could tell that we were in a family crisis. He kept going to piano lessons, church, choir rehearsal, and football camps. Only blessings for my son came out of my mouth. Nothing negative came out of my mouth, no fear speech. I prayed for the school officials, the accuser, and any other enemies that were after my son.

Why didn't I feel better immediately after the victory at the hearing? Well, I've learned some horrible things about people in this world that we live in. Be careful of who you associate with. The girl that falsely accused my son was his friend, only she wanted to be his girlfriend. He already had a girlfriend. He knew she was weird. He knew she had electro-shock therapy. He knew she had a mental problem and he kept associating with her. I taught my kids to embrace especially those people who had problems, disabilities, or were teased by others, so I'm not surprised that he was friends with this disturbed girl. But, I was shocked when I heard her lie at the hearing and accuse my son. She lied so well. There was no regard for the consequences to my son. The school district's lawyer did his job. He made a wonderful case against my son, even though he knew he was not guilty. Anybody with half a brain would know, but he was obligated to do his job, right?

I feel better now. My Christian counselor, Miss Nelly got me through it all. Two weeks ago she noticed that I stopped complaining about my marriage and my husband. I was functioning, but preoccupied. My sister told me that I didn't look like I was going through something this summer, but now I'm wreck. It's all over now and I'm a wreck. I had the spirit of courage during the trial and when it was over, all of the emotions that I repressed with faith and courage exploded.

I've burst into tears several times since this all began but not in front of my son until after he was cleared by the police a week ago. I even thought about drinking alcohol again. Of course I didn't but the feeling inside of me was bothering me and I remembered how alcohol could ease the anxiety. In my family growing up alcohol was the antidote to all that ailed. My maternal grandmother was an alcoholic. My maternal grandfather binge drank on the weekends. Their kids became alcoholics and drug addicts. In our family the only way to have a good time was with the aid of alcohol or drugs. Certainly, a bad day or stress was treated with alcohol.

When I was 15 years old my parents let us have Manischewitz wine for thanksgiving. We were allowed to drink wine coolers. Of course this turned into drinking beer and hard liquor. By the time I got to medical school, I was drinking vodka every day. The glasses got taller and taller. Thank God I stopped drinking alcohol during both pregnancies, but I returned to drinking once I finished breastfeeding. Regrettably, I also drove my car under the influence of alcohol. I never had an accident or hurt anybody or got caught, only by the grace and mercy of God.

All along, in my spirit, I dreamed of not drinking alcohol. I was impressed by people who at parties said, "I don't drink." I wanted to be able to say that too but I didn't know how. Finally, when my baby son was two years old and my daughter was six years old, I decided that they would be okay if I left them with my husband to go on my church's women's retreat. I'll never forget then Sister McEllis (now she's Reverend) preached on having a hunger and a thirst for the word of God. My life has never been the same. She told us to lift our hands to God and pray for a hunger and a thirst for God's word and I did. I was happy to do it. When I got home I bought a new bible and started reading it every day. I started going to church on time, instead of 15 minutes late and I stopped drinking alcohol.

When people ask me why I stopped drinking alcohol I tell them because it is what God wanted me to do. It is part of my witness for God. Alcohol has been and still is incredibly destructive in my family and I was on my way to being an alcoholic like my sister and brothers. It wasn't easy being around my family and not drinking. I used to bring the Absolut Vodka. My mother, my sister and I would socialize and drink together all the time. Our fellowship together centered around a big bottle of Absolut. When I stopped drinking, they mourned the loss of their drinking buddy. They talked about me behind my back. They made comments about how I was going to go back to drinking. When I would have a difficult problem, my mom suggested, have a drink. I never did and I never will. It takes the spirit of courage to stand out from your loved ones and trust God to solve your problems.

Drinking alcohol is a terrible way to solve problems. Everything suffers from that strategy, the liver, the brain, relationships, job performance, etc. It is interesting how my mother introduced me to two ways to handle problems: drinking or singing. As it turns out, there is a scripture that also addresses these two ways of dealing with difficulties.

> *Do not get drunk on wine, which leads to debauchery. Instead, be filled with the Spirit, [19] speaking to one another with psalms, hymns, and songs from the Spirit. Sing and make music from your heart to the Lord, [20] always giving thanks to God the Father for everything, in the name of our Lord Jesus Christ.*
>
> —EPHESIANS 5:18-20

As far as I can remember, singing has always been a very important part of my life. My mother used to sing all the time around the house. The record player would be blasting and she would be singing while cleaning the house or cooking. This encouraged me to sing and sing loud as there was nothing ever quiet about our house.

I loved to sing with my mother. Her love for me was clear and apparent when we were singing. We would sing Mahalia Jackson songs around the house with passion. It brought such joy to our home. She would say, "Sing it Turk!" (Turkey is my nickname, maybe I'll explain later.) I sang even louder, from my gut, because I knew she liked it. For me it was an expression of my love for my mother and her love for me. I sang in the church choir from early childhood, at Boston University during college, and at Faith Baptist Church currently.

I sang to my husband when we were falling in love, then to my children when they were babies. I serenaded my first born with the song, "You are my Sunshine." We would be at my mother's house and if Amanda was crying or upset I would start singing and made everybody else sing to her. There was nothing that would stop me from singing to my precious baby, I loved her so much I just had to sing about it. She loved it!

When I read the bible cover to cover and came across Zephaniah 3:17, I was amazed. God feels the same way that I do about singing. Or more correctly, I got it from God. God expresses God's love through singing too.

> *The LORD your God is with you,*
> *the Mighty Warrior who saves.*
> *He will take great delight in you;*
> *in his love he will no longer rebuke you,*
> *but will rejoice over you with singing.*
>
> —ZEPHANIAH 3:17

SPIRIT OF COURAGE

Having the spirit of courage and singing sounds good and doable until a really bad problem comes. It is interesting how we get used to problems and how we manage them. But when a new kind of really bad problem comes along it knocks us off our foundation. The thought of my son being arrested, put in detention, going on trial, having a criminal record for something that he did not do was not comprehendible to me. Especially since I have been praying for my son since before he was born.

My son is a product of me, God, and my husband. When I realized that my beautiful baby boy was going to be a Black man in the United States, I cried and I prayed. I have laid my hands on his head and prayed so much for him that it is just a part of our relationship. Whenever I lay my hands on his head, he just stops and receives it. Both my kids do, but I do it much more for my son then for my daughter because he is a Black man in the United States. One day Reverend Glenda asked my son about what his mother, who is a doctor, would do if he gets sick. He said, "she would just pray over me." Technically, that's not what a doctor is suppose to do when someone is sick, but that's what I do. I've got anointing oil too! When I learned about anointing oil and its properties and power, I started smearing it on my kids heads, my husband's head and my head.

The spirit of courage that keeps me going even when I'm asking God, "Why?" comes from Christ. Praying keeps me going, singing keeps me going, but most of all knowing that I am triumphant in Christ keeps me going. This means that as I follow the ways of Christ, the will of God always wins.

Lessons Learned and Reflection Questions

1. Reflect on your childhood. No matter the circumstances know that you are seen and heard by God if Jesus Christ is your Lord and Savior. Are you seen and heard by God?

2. Alcohol, marijuana, narcotics, cocaine, etc. do not solve the problems of life. They temporarily take away anxiety, but the problem is still there.

3. How do you solve your problems?

4. What does triumphant in Christ mean to you?

TWO

The Truth Shall Set You Free

Sleep is a natural state of bodily rest. The body rests while the mind is unaware and not on. It makes sense, body and mind in sync. We usually sleep quite comfortably in darkness. But when we are awake, there is usually light. Certainly this is how it was in ancient times when there was not street lights or flood lights or skylines. There was no work going on in the dark. It was time to be quiet, rest, and sleep.

Some people are afraid of the dark. They also may be afraid to go to sleep because of nightmares. I wonder if insomnia was a problem in ancient times. With no lamp, no television, or computer to spend the time, what other choices were there? God did make is so that we can have sex quite nicely in the dark.

But what are we avoiding in 2012 when the lights are always on? Times Square in NYC is always open and lit up like a Christmas tree. There are so many lights, it is probably the safest place on earth. Now the nightmare occurs during daylight. We are afraid of the light of the day. We are afraid of the truth. We are avoiding the truth. All truth. We remain in the darkness of denial, avoidance and secrecy. Where's the relief? Waking up to the new day provides light. Acknowledging the truth brings relief and freedom.

Slavery was a nightmare, not only for African Americans, but for the entire United States of America. It stopped more than a century ago, but the United States continues to suffer from the consequences of slavery because of secrecy and cover-up. The idea is if we forget, cover-up, hide and keep secret, the ugliness will disappear. The stench of the tragedy will be invisible. But the problem is that people don't forget the hurt, cover-ups get uncovered, and secrets get revealed. It takes courage for someone to reveal secrets. That is what I am doing with this book. I am releasing all kinds of family secrets. Not to hurt anybody, but to release everybody.

Release from the shame of thinking that I am worse than everybody else, so if I keep it to myself and nobody will know and I won't have to be embarrassed. No everybody has skeletons in their closets. I, Miss Perfect, have a whole slew of them. There is nobody in the world who can make me feel bad because of my history or my family's history. They have a history too, they just aren't sharing.

One of my mother's Godly revelations to me was about secrets. She told me don't keep secrets. It makes things worse. It's ironic that she told me that considering all of the secrets she has kept from me and my siblings regarding our parents' infidelities, breakup, divorce, custody, and child support. Not only did she keep secrets, she influenced our thinking about our father and his love and concern for us in a negative way. My father chose not to set the record straight until a few years ago when my sister and I were having breakfast with him one day. We still don't know the whole story but he is not the monster my mother played him out to be.

I wholeheartedly recommend busting up secrets and letting the chips fall where they may. Generational curses would disappear if people would do this. There is freedom in the truth. Surely Christians know that there is freedom in Christ Jesus. ("To the Jews who had believed him, Jesus said, If you hold to my teaching, you are really my disciples. Then you will know the truth, and the truth will set you free." John 8:31-32) Christians have the leverage of Christ to heal the realities of the truth and the consequences of secrets.

I believe there is healing in history. The knowledge of history gives the opportunity to change the future. It is a horrible, selfish thing for parents to actively or passively give their children the oppressions and addictions of their ancestors. Why pass on this death and destruction to the children? We need to do better and I am, will you?

The problem is who knows who my ancestors were? My maternal grandmother had a white, Jewish father and a black mother. My great grandmother was raped and got pregnant with my grandmother. Nana was raised by her aunt. She could most assuredly pass for a white woman, but she didn't. She was Black. At age 13 she married a very brown Black man who my mom says was very handsome. This was in the 1930s. I don't have many details for you about their marriage because on the day he was killed Nana told her 10 children not to ever mention his name again. I think she killed him, but Uncle Nokey took the blame and went to reform school. I think he was 13 years old. The powers that be determined that Nana needed to stay home and take care of the children. Supposedly this secret was for the families good?

The other secret was that my grandfather who I never met beat Nana every Friday night. The same thing every week over and over again. He'd get paid good money from the cleaners, go to a club and get drunk and lose all the money gambling and come home to his wife and 10 kids with no money for food, clothing, bills, or whatever. So she probably killed him in self defense, only in those days wife beating was normal accepted behavior that did not require defense.

My mother says that her father really loved her. She didn't think her mother ever loved her, ever. But she knew her father loved her, and he was gone and she couldn't even grieve over him properly. My mother was 16 years old when her father was killed at the hand of her mother. Within a year my mother's favorite brother, GuGu died in a car accident after the prom. She was devastated and I believe my mother to this day never got over these two huge losses.

My older brother was born a year later. My mother was dating my father and they broke up. They got back together and my mother got pregnant. In those days, they had to get married. My mom still had to clean Nana's house even though she was married. Two years later my older sister was born and then me 15 months later and then my younger brother 2 years after that. Four kids in five years. Alcohol, infidelity, and domestic violence lead to divorce. I always thought it was my father's fault, but that was not the truth.

It's horrible being an afraid little girl. The stomach feeling full, the heart pounding, the throat constricted. Why won't they stop? Why won't she shut up? I was four or five years old when I saw my father beat my mother while she was bathing in the tub. My mother had several Black eyes in those days. So when she asked us if we wanted her to stay married to Daddy or be with Freddie, we chose Freddie because we thought there would be peace and harmony if Mommy and Daddy were apart. Even though I loved my Daddy, I hated that feeling of being afraid. So we moved to Long Island, New York to live with Freddie.

I can't be totally upset about being separated from my father and his side of the family because if we stayed in Connecticut, I would have never met the love of my life, Eric. But divorce is a big loss and all that is lost is not recoverable. Relationships with my father's side of the family suffered tremendously because of divorce. Now after all these years, we are polite strangers, more or less. I tried to make it more but it didn't work.

With this horrendous family background, what could one expect of a little girl called Turkey? Yes, my mother gave me the knick name Turkey because when she looked at me in the crib I looked like a perfect, brown, Butterball Turkey. Those closest to me call me that even today. That is what they call me, but God calls me Daughter.

God was with me from the beginning. From before the beginning of Creation, God knew all about me. I always knew that I was special. I always knew that there was some protective force around me. Now I know that that force is the Holy Spirit. My oldest brother, Dingy says that ever since I was a little girl he has seen a shining light or an aura of light around me. People tell me that all of the time. Dr. Brisbane just told me that again today. She says it is clear that I belong to God. I thank God because I know it is not about me, it is a gift from God.

The reason that I was able to overcome such a tragic family history is because I was a part of God's greater plan of spreading the Gospel within this family and to the world. I have the favor of God. People just liked me and gravitated toward me. Teachers always liked me and I always liked learning so I always did well.

In the midst of the chaos, I was raised to be respectful, polite, responsible, and independent. My mother raised her girls to be able to take care of themselves. Well, maybe that is what I learned because I was always at her feet. Val was hanging out. I was present to overhear conversations my mother had with her female friends during get-togethers. In the days of "children should be seen and not heard" I was in the presence of a bunch of Black women, listening to all sorts of dilemmas that plagued women. I also came up with ideas on how I was going to prevent all of these problems. All this crap did not have to happen to me. I had a knack for learning from other peoples experiences even at such a young age.

When I was in sixth grade our middle school had classrooms without walls and round tables. One day I was at a table by myself across from a table of 3 white girls. These were the 3 popular girls, the smart girls, the pretty girls that I wanted to be with and like. They always got A's. I got B's but I wanted to get A's. That day changed my life. I saw them pass papers between them. We were taking a test and they were cheating! I said to myself, "Ok, ok, ok, they aren't better than me. They are cheating. I am going to get A's without cheating." From that day forward, I got A's all the time. Throughout high school, college, medical school, and even 20 years later in seminary. That was the beginning of seeing the truth of things.

It is wonderful when the truth of things is revealed and one is able to see it. Even better is that I responded to the truth in an honorable way. I could have decided to cheat too. Maybe if I had a posy I would have but I was alone. I was not popular, I had no friends, I had no one to hang out with. But I could have cheated by myself. The point is that I had enough goodness in me, confidence in me to make the right choice.

Another right choice was choosing not to cheat on my boyfriend. I chose not to have sex with other men when Eric was in Atlanta. I was close twice, but I said no. I was 17, they were in college. They were friends. We met at Brookhaven National Lab. I got a job in the Medical Department after school. One worked during the summer and the other for a year. They gave me rides home. One night I went to a party with one of them and I decided to go back to his room. Somehow I ended up in his room on his couch and him trying to take off my clothes. I said no, he was heavy, thank God he got up. It was difficult. I asked him to take me home and he did and the friendship was over. I put myself in such danger. Not necessarily murder, but certainly date rape. I can see how that could have easily happened to me.

Me and Mommy were in the Volvo sitting in the driveway. She used the screwdriver to turn off the ignition and I asked her what she thought about me having sex with this guy since Eric was in Atlanta. She knew I was sexually active with Eric. She knew I was on the pill so that wasn't the issue. My mother always said the worst thing that could happen to a young woman is to get pregnant before she wanted to. Not AIDS, or any other STD, just getting pregnant. So she told me and Val to tell her before we had sex so she could bring us to the health center to get on the pill.

She said, "don't do it, it's not a good idea, it would ruin everything, it causes too much trouble, don't do it." Now I think I know why. That is what ruined her first marriage. It was her infidelity, not my father's. So I listened to my mother and I've only had sexual encounters with Eric. Not only is this pleasing to me and to my husband, but most of all it is pleasing to God.

My mom told the Godly truth. That is not her typical behavior. She usually pushes sexual immorality. She saw her mother shack up with a man and give birth to 3 babies out of wedlock. Nana was pregnant every time my mother was pregnant. This was scandalous. I thought we were special. We have an aunt Val's age, we have an aunt my age, and we have an uncle my little brother, Popie's age. We grew up together. We had fun, but my mother was embarrassed.

My mother's brothers, my uncles were pimps and brought prostitutes into their mother's home while we were there. Nana took money from her son's earnings from sex work and selling drugs. So for my mother to tell me not to be unfaithful to Eric, was certainly a Godly moment.

These Godly moments with my mother have occurred often over the years but I have noticed that they only occur when we are alone. When my other siblings are present, she is not capable of this Godliness. Rather she's probably capable, just not willing. I'm surrounded by people not willing to surrender to God. Not willing to tell the truth. Not willing to look back and reflect on their lives. Not willing to change and do better. I used to be this way too but not anymore. Let me re-phrase, I tried to be not willing to be the person God called me to be on purpose.

I tried to be like my sister. Popular, hip, cool, having a lot of friends and boys after her. It didn't work. I've tried to be like so many people in my life because there always seemed to be something wrong with me, according to other people. I always thought about things differently from other people. I am hard to take. I'm intimidating. Now I know, its not my problem its their problem. But I still have to have enough courage and confidence to be who God created me to be even if I am rejected by people, especially friends and family. It's not me they are running away from, it is God they are running from. How stupid to try to run away from God. A waste of time and energy that's never gonna work.

God has always been good to me to send me people to help me stay on this road he has prepared for me. People who could see the specialness in me gave me special treatment back. They treated me like I was their favorite compared to others. People might say I am a professional "brown noser" but I was just trying to do the right thing because I really wanted to or I was compelled to out of wisdom. Or maybe I was trying to be perfect so that someone would love me. The truth is the more perfect I became, the less people liked me. The more I would do right in the eyes of God, the harder I was to be around.

I drank alcohol because that was the normal and expected thing to do. It is not normal not to drink alcohol. You can't have fun if you don't drink alcohol at a social event. If you have a hard day, the popular answer is to get a drink. The problem is that the alcohol never solved a problem. The same thing can be said for drugs. Marijuana made things feel better, unless you become paranoid. But with my family history, drinking alcohol is the key to death and destruction.

My grandfather was a binge alcoholic, my grandmother was an alcoholic, my mother is an alcoholic, my brother is an alcoholic, my sister is an alcoholic, therefore, I concluded I am an alcoholic too. Genetically that is. God had been telling me for years to stop drinking alcohol. It was a feeling inside. I would admire people, especially women who would say, "I don't drink alcohol." But I would still buy my big bottle of Absolut and I would drink it all by myself. Eric drank beer. Every day after working in the operating room 10 hours giving anesthesia I would be exhausted emotionally and physically. I would get a tall glass, 12-16 oz and put vodka, diet coke, orange juice, grapefruit juice, something split 50-50, then the ice. I would lay in my bed and put it on the night stand and drink it until I fell asleep. I was able to function. Give the children baths, read them stories, put them to bed. My husband always cooked. I was functioning, we were okay but that was not what God had planned for us.

I drank alcohol with my mother. I learned how to drink from her. She drank vodka, so I drank vodka. Nana drank vodka too. I just was able to buy top shelf vodka. My family looked forward to me bringing it to family gatherings.

Drinking is one thing, but the fights that broke out because of alcohol intoxication is a whole other dimension. Ugly, ugly, ugly. The verbal attacks. Even physical violence. Every physical fight my mother ever had with my father, Willie her lover, or Pop was bathed in alcohol. Every black eye and bruise had the smell of alcohol all over it. She did not shut up because she was drunk. She kept verbally attacking these men's manhood because she was drunk. And because they were drunk, they hit her. It kept happening over and over and over again. Until they got too old and it became ridiculous to them. But the only thing that stopped was the physical violence. The verbal abuse continues.

I did the same thing in my marriage. My mother always said "the apple doesn't fall far from the tree." My 13 year old son added this nuance to the proverb, "unless the tree is on a hill." That tree is the Mount of Zion, where our help comes from. The tree is God. The tree is the cross. In other words, because of Jesus we have been set free from the bondages and curses of our ancestors.

If the lies and secrets continue, the generational curses continue. I love my kids and future descendents too much to allow this spiritual decadence to continue. Who knows what happened to the women before Nana? But I do know that Nana suffered. I know that my mother suffered. I know that I have suffered. But that's where it stops in the name of Jesus! The lies have stopped. The secrets have stopped. The devil has been defeated, way back on the cross. This suffering is not necessary. Jesus already paid the price.

Jesus already paid the price so that we don't have to believe the lies of alcoholism, drug addiction, sexual immorality, domestic violence, and poverty. It is so easy, all we have to do is believe it and receive it. My mother still thinks that all of the above is normal behavior that cannot be overcome. God help her. I told her she needs Jesus and yesterday I told her she needs therapy.

Lessons Learned and Reflection Questions

1. Truth shall set you free.

2. Don't let the devil accuse you, be honest with God and tell all of your secrets.

3. Write down your family secrets.

4. Keep a journal about your feelings of bitterness and frustration regarding your past.

5. Don't keep generational curses alive.

6. Have you forgave yourself for your past mistakes?

7. Have you forgiven others for their mistakes?

THREE

The Ups and Downs of Abundant Living

In this past four years we have seen fluctuations in the stock market, election polls, the electoral map, people switching from being democrat to republican or republican to independent. People are afraid of their future. This is measured by the fall in the stock market. There are emotions associated with the ups and downs of living. People are losing confidence in the false security they had in the words "United States of America." People are changing their minds about their ideas about "colored people" or people from the mid-western , people from the south, people from Alaska, basically just people different from them.

Life is about change, some good some bad, some up and some down. From the time we are born until we die there will be ups and downs. There are ups and downs in my son's football games, my daughter's moods, my husband's pain in his feet and my patient's blood pressures and heart rates. To me, life is like a long rollercoaster ride.

People are afraid. There are times when certain people are afraid and others are not. The citizens of the US might be afraid of different things than people in the Sudan or Haiti. They might be afraid of starving to death whereas we might be worried about missing 1 meal in the day. They might be worried about finding shelter each and every day and we are worried about our wide screen TV not working. And what about Black parents in the US afraid that their children will be discriminated against, oppressed, treated unfairly, or even killed. Do parents of white 14 year old boys in the US teach their sons how to behave *when* they are confronted by police? Do parents of white 14 year old boys tell their sons not to run from police in fear of their babies being shot in the back. Gunned down for no reason other than being Black.

How does an African American family in the US have joy in the face of the reality that their children, especially their sons, have a much higher risk of being murdered or put in jail just because some person judged them based on lies about people with brown skin? Of course we don't like it, but it is a part of life in the US. It's unfair and tragic foolishness. But I am sure that white people would have their own ideas of unfair and tragic foolishness in the US. They are allowed. Each person is able to identify their own hurts and oppression. It is oppressive to tell someone that their hurts are not valid. It is a trick of the devil to pit one person or group of people against another. No sense in grading your hurts worse or more painful than another's. By definition, if a person is breathing, he or she faces the difficulties and stresses of life.

No matter who you are or where you live life is full of ups and downs. There are good times and there are bad times. There are times when you are going up and other times when you are going down. The question is not how you feel during these phases, but how you behave?

There is also a speed factor involved. We could be creeping up ever so slowly and crawling down feeling our way. Or we can be mounting eagle's wings and soaring up and then we can be in freefall like there was a huge anchor tied around our necks.

This is what it means to be alive. And this is what circumstances are. Circumstances go up and down. Things in life just don't stay the same. I think this is what people are afraid of.

People want reassurances. We want guarantees that while we are crawling or soaring up that we won't fall. We don't even want to look down. We are afraid and it makes us feel uncomfortable, right in the pit of our stomachs.

It reminds me of rollercoasters. My reaction to rollercoasters. I don't ride rollercoasters anymore. I have never enjoyed them and I really tried. I tried because everybody else in the family or group of friends loved them! I wanted to be a part of the fun. I wanted to fit in. The ride would always start slow. Harmless, those who like them would call it boring. But for me I would be in a sea of terror. Wondering why did I do this again. I would consider getting off as the car crept up the incline, I looked to one side and saw the rest of the ride, I looked to the other side and saw the small steps. These steps seemed like they were there for me. And I seriously thought I could get out and climb down, anything would be better than going down that bid drop. I was terrified but quiet. Me quiet, that lets you know something isn't right! But most of the other people were screaming. They seemed like they couldn't wait to go down. Like that was the best part of the ride. I still don't understand that.

This is what life is like. Ups and downs. Joy and Terror. Apprehension and uncertainty. Not knowing whether to stay in the car and endure the scary ride or risk getting out of the car and falling, or falling off the steps while climbing down. It was a horrible feeling. At the same time that I felt terror, I felt downright stupid. Why did I keep doing this to myself? I don't enjoy this so why was I doing it? I was doing it because everybody else was doing it. I went to the amusement park with friends and family and I wanted to be with them and have fun like them. I was trying to be like them and force myself to enjoy what they enjoyed even though I knew I would not enjoy it.

This is the story of my young life. Always trying to get joy from what others did knowing that I did not enjoy it but thinking something was wrong with me because I didn't enjoy it and the truth is that I was not supposed to. God created me from the foundation of the world to be different from everybody else! It is a hard thing for a young person to embrace especially when surrounded by a family like mine. A family where evil behaviors where considered normal and unforgiveness and envy were the prevailing attitudes. For sure the devil had a vested interest in me believing and living these lies. I was raised in the bondage of these lies. But, I knew something was wrong. I would even say it.

I would get in trouble for telling adults that they were wrong, not telling the truth, not being fair, and immoral. I knew I had to get away. When I fell in love with Eric, I thought that was my escape from evil. Actually at around the same time I was falling in love with Eric, I was also falling in love with Jesus. I did except Jesus Christ as my LORD and Savior when I was 17 years old, but now I know I was more in love with Eric.

If you want to know who Tracie is in love with, check out my songs. Who am I singing too? And the singing I am talking about is loud and coming from the gut. From the time I met Eric until I gave birth to Amanda, I sang to Eric. When I gave birth to Amanda, I sang to her. I have been in church choirs since I was a little girl, but the singing was not an expression of love. It was something else. My mother made us go to Sunday school and sing in the choir, but she did not go to church with us. I thank God that she knew enough to make us go although when we got to be teenagers she stopped forcing us. I went on my own because Eric was forced by his mother to go to church every Sunday.

After I had my son, I started singing in the choir again. That is when I started singing love songs to God. I was still singing to the children, but I was done singing to Eric. I was too hurt. He betrayed me. My father, through divorce, abandoned me. I was better than my mother in terms of knowing and doing the right thing so she resented me and did not encourage me in any good way. She would say hurtful things like, "you are so smart you have no common sense." Yet look at my life. Look how successful I have been. I have plenty of common sense. "You are so smart you are stupid." In my heart I knew better. But it hurt. There is no hurt like the hurt from your mother. My mother knew this because her mother hurt her. Why do we keep hurting our children from generation to generation?

Being hurt by your parents and grandparents is definitely a down. Nana didn't like me because I didn't believe her lies and I would say so. She knew that I was not a loyal follower of hers. And there were a lot of loyal followers. I couldn't understand it. My mother was so afraid of this little old woman. She hurt my mother up until she died and my mother never told her the truth. She was afraid. I even offered to tell Nana myself and my mother said no. I was angry with Nana because she didn't love me and she hurt my mother.

I wish I knew Nana's story. I'm sure her childhood was horrendous. How does she end up getting married at age 13. The secrets died with her. None of her kids had the courage to get the information. I can only surmise that it was worse than my mother's but with the same themes: alcoholism, sexual immorality, unforgiveness, envy, lying, cheating, stealing and murder. All right up the devil's alley! In order for me to be able to have abundant living, I had to forgive Nana, but it wasn't easy and I didn't want to.

God has given each of us lives to live and it is our duty to live life to the fullest. Each minute is precious, each breath is a miracle. Why do we think that we have to get what we want for life to be good? Where did we get the idea that life would be perfect, except for being in Christ Jesus? Tents go up before dusk and at dawn tents come down. One year there are floods the next drought. One year heat waves the next a deep freeze. How do we reconcile in our minds the ups and downs of living? How do we think about living the abundant life in the midst of ups and downs?

The truth of the matter is that at any given point in our lives, we are pressed on every side, from within and without, by problems, troubles, difficulties, conflicts, frustrations, and disappointments. We are perplexed, we don't know why God would allow suffering. Especially the suffering of the innocent 20 first graders that were gunned down in their classrooms at Sandy Hook Elementary School. We are hunted down and knocked down but we can't give up, we are not abandoned by God and we have to keep going. (2 Corinthians 4)

So how do we handle suffering, falling, dipping and diving? We rely on the same power that raised up Jesus Christ, to raise us back up. Jesus voluntarily was flogged, whipped, spit on, stabbed and allowed to bleed and suffocate to death while being nailed to a cross. We must be able to relate to what happened to Jesus when we are falling, dying, bleeding and suffocating as well. We must allow the resurrection power that raised up Jesus Christ to raise us up. God is able to raise up. No matter how far down we go, God's hand can reach down and pick us up. How do you behave when God reaches down and picks you up? You praise God in every way you can. Praise God before, during, and after God picks you up.

One late summer Saturday morning the phone rang. My 85 year old sick grandmother from Connecticut is getting worse in the hospital. In my spirit, I know that I need to get to my Nana. This is going to be the last time we get to see her alive. Hurricane "Henry" is coming up the coast toward Long Island. My husband has to work. I have to get us to Connecticut.

Driving to the Port Jefferson Ferry, my two kids and I notice the sun trying to peek through the clouds. The water at the dock looked calm. We climbed the stairs to the boat's cabin. The children headed straight for the food bar. The boat rocked as we were getting condiments. It was no big deal. We've traveled across the Long Island Sound to Bridgeport many times before. This time the waves were particularly rough. We walked slowly, balancing our food and drinks. The boat rocked up and down. We had to hold on to the table, tight.

I was scared. This was worse than ever before.

I wanted to cry, but I couldn't. My kids wanted to cry, but they didn't. I looked into their eyes and I knew I had to do something to help them. I said, "Everything is going to be alright kids, let's pray." Immediately we held hands and I prayed out loud: "Dear Heavenly Father, we thank you for everything Lord. We know Lord that you are in control of everything on earth and in heaven. Please cover us and this boat with the blood of Jesus. Bless the captain and his crew to steer this boat over these waves. Please help us to get to Connecticut safely. Hallelujah, thank you Jesus, Amen." They echoed, "Amen."

I said to the children, "Let's sing praise songs kids. Come on let's sing out loud!"

> "This is the day, this is the day, that the Lord has made, that the Lord had made, I will rejoice, I will rejoice, and be glad in it, and be glad in it. This is the day that the Lord has made, I will rejoice and be glad in it. This is the day, this is the day that the Lord has made."

The ferry continued to rock and roll over the huge angry waves. As we gripped the table, we kept singing. There was loud crying all around us. Bam! Clang! An elderly man tumbled to the floor. A garbage can tipped over, it rolled across the cabin floor.

I knew that we were going to get to Bridgeport alive, I just didn't know if it was going to be by the ferry or by the coastguard plucking us out of the water by helicopter. We kept singing.

> "I will enter his gates with thanksgiving in my heart, I will enter his courts with praise, I will say this is the day that the Lord has made, I will rejoice for He has made me glad."

Thank God, the rocking got lighter. We could see Bridgeport. We made it. Hallelujah, Thank you Jesus. My Nana was barely alive when I got in her room in the intensive care unit. My mother says she was waiting for me to get there. When I got to her bedside she had shallow breathing but seemed to respond to me when I called her name. I squeezed her hand and I tried to pray but I couldn't. I was overwhelmed with emotion and words could not come out. Thank God for my aunt Sharon, she started praying and Nana died. This was one year before I would accept the call to the Gospel ministry.

To my stomach, the ups and downs of the ferry felt like the ups and downs of a rollercoaster. When I was riding roller coasters I did not sing through it. The fear overwhelmed me. I thank God that I know now to sing my way through the ups and downs of life in the spirit of courage.

Lessons Learned

1. Life is full of ups and downs.

2. God lifts us up.

3. Sing praises to God while life is rocking and rolling. If you don't sing, dance, paint, write poems, plant a garden, volunteer to help those in need, call a lonely person, smile… … …

FOUR

Taking Care and Care Taking

From the beginning of accepting the call to ministry, I vowed that I would not be a "stumbling block" along other's journeys to seek, find, and follow Jesus Christ. I call it "Do No Harm," from the Hippocratic Oath I took when I graduated from medical school. Similarly, just like it is unacceptable for people to practice medicine without training, I believe that clergy should not practice ministry without proper training, along with being called by God. No human being calls a person to ministry or to preach the Gospel, it must come from God.

I have been called by God to be a physician and a minister. More specifically, I have been called to a three-fold pastoral ministry of teaching, preaching and healing. Ministry is done by using the tools that God gives through grace that will help effectively minister to and serve oppressed, hurting people. Effective ministry is liberating, healing, life-changing and life-sustaining. What is the use of preaching and teaching ministries that don't transform lives so that people are free to enjoy abundant living?

It is imperative that I not only preach and teach about Christ and the love of God, but also about living healthy, Godly lifestyles. God's people need to be educated and know the truth about their health and the consequences of their lifestyles. For example, eating healthy diets, regular exercise, abstinence from sex outside of marriage and avoidance of alcohol and drugs are very important behaviors that should be encouraged from pulpits.

We have to get rid of the idea that it is not appropriate to talk about things such as HIV/AIDS, alcoholism, domestic violence or sex in church. It is a trick of the devil to keep these things secret only to be discussed with whispers, behind closed doors. Christians have such a problem talking about and hearing about sex in general, let alone church. God created sex, it was God's idea. God chose to make us sexual beings. God chose for us to procreate through sex, God chose to make our bodies to have the ability to have sexual pleasure. Sex was God's design and we should stop the tradition of making sex dirty and unholy.

There should be sex workshops in church that focus on our attitudes about God ordained uses of the body. The goal is to get people talking about their health, sex, and self-control. Christian clergy need teach men, women, boys and girls what God says about them, their health, sex, and their bodies. The HIV/AIDS epidemic in the African American community will only get better when we start talking and stop pretending about our sexualities.

When it comes to ministry, pretending is never a good thing, no matter who is doing the pretending or what the pretending is about. One of the "Aha" moments for me during seminary is that ministry is more about the way things are and less about the way things should be. It is very important to minister in reality. Reality as in what *really* and *truly* is going on. The reality of situations is gained through the help of the Holy Spirit. Christian clergy must seek the Holy Spirit not only to gain wisdom about caring for others, but also just as important for self-care.

In order to be able to do effective ministry in this complicated world self-care is critical. Self-care is ministry-saving so that it's okay to take a day off in ministry. Self-care is sacred pampering, holy, and sacrificial, it's not secondary. But it takes courage to set limits and boundaries that may disappoint those who we minister to and serve.

Sacred pampering allows me to love God, my neighbor and myself according to the Greatest Commandment noted in both testaments of the bible (Leviticus 19:18, *Mark 12:28-34, Luke 10:25-28, Matthew 7:12, 19:19, 22:34-40, Romans 13:9* and *Galatians 5:14*) . Through sacred pampering I am cooperating with God to love myself, to be my best, and to be available to others for their healing. My goal is to always remember my oath to "Do No Harm." The last thing the world needs is another cranky clergy person who hurts people.

This is a major challenge for those who multitask because multi-taskers sometimes run out of time and get cranky. With God's guidance, I must manage my time with wisdom. I continue to purge my schedule and block additions to it unless I hear from God otherwise. I must regularly get enough sleep, exercise, and not eat too much. The best ways to prevent stress is to bask in God's rest, meditate on God's word, and listen for God's counsel.

The manifestations of God's faithfulness are energizing. Ministry requires expectation, structure and discipline. Running a ministry is the same as running a home or an operating room. My family has always been very busy structured around school, work, and church. Homework gets done every night and my kids are expected to do their best to get A's and B's. We go to Sunday school and church every Sunday. Operating rooms are structured around patient safety, patient satisfaction, and efficiency.

TAKING CARE AND CARE TAKING

Ministry must be structured around the love of people. Every aspect of a person's life can be ministered to. There are no aspects of life that God is not the center, the question is will we even let God in the circle let alone the center. Ministers of the Gospel are in the business of service to people wherever we find them; at home, at work, the street, the park, on the train and in church.

I love God with all my heart and I take Jesus with me where ever I go. This is a part of my ministry. My faith in God is part of my armamentaria as a physician for practicing anesthesiology. Every day I pray for my patients and the whole operating room staff. I learned very quickly in may practice of anesthesiology that I needed more than my excellent medical training to care for my patients. On several occasions in the operating room when my patients were not doing well and the medical team was doing everything we knew to do, I would pray for healing and restoration. God is faithful and God always answers my prayers. I believe that my professional success is a gift from God. I have the gift of healing hands and I honor the gift when prompted by the Holy Spirit.

Recently when I went to work at the hospital I found out that one of my colleagues suffered a massive heart attack. He is a forty-four year old husband and father of two young sons. He is a man that I have had confrontational problems in the past and thankfully have been resolved. I went to the Cardiac Care Unit to see him and as I walked in his room, his wife stood up and walked toward me and reached out her hand to me. I took her hand and embraced her sideways. We walked to the bedside and I took his hand in mine briefly. He had a breathing tube coming out of his mouth connected to a ventilator and heavily sedated so he didn't really need me, but she clearly did. I sat, held her hand, listened, and nodded.

This is one of the most valuable things I learned from Professor Jones during seminary! It's how to be pastoral. I did not pray out loud, but I never stopped praying. I prayed before, during, and after the visit, just me and God. She did not ask for me to pray and I did not volunteer. Thank God my colleague is got better and is back to work. Sitting, holding hands, listening, (prayerful) silence, and nodding really works.

Ministry works not only from the work of the Holy Spirit, but from other earthly resources. Two people were my special resources for ministry: my pastor, Reverend Dr. Beresford Adams and my Field Education supervisor, Dr. Frances Brisbane. The most important thing Dr. Brisbane taught me was that every event is an opportunity to minister to someone. Make each moment in ministry impact experiences for those being served.

In September 2008, heaven allowed Dr. Brisbane, another multitasker, to be able to come to Union to the Field Education Supervisor's Meeting. At the end of Chapel service she gave me a rock and told me to keep it with me always and when things get too hard for me to stand it, to squeeze the rock as hard as I can. I should always know that just like I can't crush the rock in my hands, whatever is challenging me also can't crush me because God is always with me. That was an impact experience for me and at the same time I learned two ways to impact others lives. One is to encourage mentees to repeat positive aphorisms about who they are and who God is. Confirm that God has anointed them and that the light of Christ lives in

TAKING CARE AND CARE TAKING

them. Two is to give them something to hold/keep/look at to remind them of the experience. The aphorisms and the keepsake continue to effectively minister well beyond the moment.

A major focus at my field site during seminary was to minister effectively young adults in such a way that lives are transformed which results in abundant living. Abundant living means positive life changes such as pursuing higher education, gameful employment, healthy lifestyles, and civic responsibility. How do you connect with a young person in some meaningful way when you only have easy access to the external portion of the person and a limited amount of time? So many times I find that people say what they think you want to hear, only giving a portion of the truth of a situation and usually the portion that makes them look good. It takes time to see even a portion of the "underwater iceberg" of a human being, so how do we help people in the mean time, with knowing only a fraction of what the true problem is? One of my friends, Melanie, who is also a Baptist minister gave me these steps for ministering to people: 1) Pray; 2) Time; 3) Patience; 4) Open mind; 5) Active listening; 6) Wait; 7) Ask God to help answer; 8) Let God speak to you.

One of my greatest challenges is being patient. I too often have unrealistic expectations about how quickly Christians should be growing in Christ. Having realistic expectations of people in ministry as well as those being ministered to is also a challenge for me. I expect a lot from myself and others. The problem is that the one thing that human beings are guaranteed to do is to disappoint, frustrate, betray and annoy. I believe this is why in the past I have considered *administration* a bad word.

On the contrary, through one of my Field Education class "Aha" moments I learned that *administration* is not a bad word. According to Christie Neuger, "Administration is the enabling and empowering dimension of a group coming to discern its need, hopes, and goals, and then coming to believe in and care for itself in such a way that it is motivated to care for and serve something beyond itself." [1] The important "Aha" I've learned is that administration encompasses the self-care of an organization. "[It] is nurturing and motivating the group to move toward ministry, toward service. Its focus is on empowering people." [2]

But, on a practical note, how does a minister keep loving people who continually betray? Why continue to minister to people who persistently disappoint? Ministers must focus on God and not the behavior of people. Focus on the mission and not the mess-up. Jesus is the only one who did not and never will fall short of my expectations. I am committed to the will of God, serving God's purpose, and preaching the Gospel of Jesus Christ. I will not relax my convictions about what I know about God because of other's disbelief. I must learn to be satisfied with progress over a life-time and not to demand or expect immediate transformation. I must remember that this is the work of the Holy Spirit and not me. God does the work. I am just the minister, mediator or intercessor.

Ministers of the Gospel have been ordained since before the foundation of the world. In other words, it was God's plan

---

[1] Christie C. Neuger, ed., *The Arts of Ministry: Feminist-Womanist Approaches* (Louisville: Westminster John Knox Press, 1996), 120.

[2] Ibid.

before we were born. God blesses God's called people with talents and gifts that are supposed to be used in ministry. This is why it would be a grave mistake to try to copy someone else's ministry. We each have unique and specialized ministries. We can get help from others but direction has to come from God.

I keep in contact with God by starting my daily routine with the Lord. The foundation of my daily devotion is from Oswald Chambers', *My Utmost for His Highest*,[3] followed by reading my Sunday school daily scriptures, and praying. This keeps me focused and gives me strength. Most of all this process helps me grow my faith and trust in God. Another thing that helps is that I am generally a happy and positive person. I purposefully cultivate the joy of the Lord in my spirit of courage.

My seminary training at Union Theological Seminary cultivated me to be able to use my God-given gifts and talents for the maximum benefit to God's people. In particular, Union's focus on diversity, pluralism and social justice prepared me to minister to all people. My Field Education experience was full of impact moments that shaped how I do ministry. My preaching, teaching, and healing ministry consists of aphorisms, keep-sakes, listening and nodding, administration and days off.

---

[3] Oswald Chambers, *My Utmost For His Highest*. (Uhrichsville: Barbour Publishing, 1963).

Lessons Learned

1. Expect the best from people but don't be shocked if they disappoint you. Only Jesus is perfect.
2. Be quick to forgive
3. Do not murder with your words

FIVE

Waging War

Judges 6:12 "When the angel of the LORD appeared to Gideon, he said, "The LORD is with you, mighty warrior."

War, battles, lies, conflicts, Jihad. There are all kinds of troubles that we have to face in a lifetime. Survival, relationships, government, legal, medical/health. The United States has been at war for over a decade, the democrats are battling for the nomination, the republicans are battling to stay in the white house, no that was in 2008. In 2012, it was the other way around. Nations make decisions about engaging in war and individuals have to decide whether or not to engage in the daily struggles of life.

It takes courage to enter into battle. It is much easier to ignore problems or step away from conflict. Pretending that problems don't exist or living in denial usually backfires. Some Christians are surprised to find out that we ought to expect to have problems and struggles throughout our lives. God expects us to trust God and walk with God as we journey through life's problems and engage in the war against evil.

I want to share with you three biblical ways God teaches us to fight war. The first thing we have to do is *identify the enemy*. "For we wrestle not against flesh and blood, but against principalities, against powers, against the rulers of the darkness of this world, against spiritual wickedness in high places." (Ephesians 6:12) Principalities are powers in conflict with God, traditions in conflict with God, ungodly mindsets, and wrong thinking. According to God's way this is what our fight is against, evil, not people, not flesh and blood.

The second step in fighting battles is to *figure out a strategy* or strategies. It is very important to have a strategy all set before going to war or fighting a battle. This reminds me of playing cards or checkers or backgammon or chess or any game with my husband. Nine times out of ten, he would always win. He always had a strategy to win while I was just playing to be with him, have fun, and smile at him.

To be honest, I didn't really consider playing games with my husband as battles or conflict or war, he took it much more seriously than I did. And that's a problem. Not for our marriage necessarily because I didn't mind if he won, I actually admired him for his skills. But in life, in this evil world we live in to walk around in La La Land of peaches and cream, peace and loveliness, is absurd. It is a beautiful sentiment but very foolish. No matter how much we want to live conflict free it is impossible. Being a human being, breathing and moving in this earth is by definition a conflict or a struggle. We have struggles at home in our families, at work with our colleagues, at church with other believers, in traffic with other cars, on airplanes with other passengers, etc. Some of us even have conflicts with God and the way God allows things to happen or not happen. Thus, we must always be ready to respond to conflicts with a targeted strategy.

But where does one get her strategy from? Christians get their strategies for battles from the word of God. The first objective is to have the proper mindset that is essential in responding to attacks from enemies. In Christ, we are triumphant in all of our battles which fulfills the declaration of the LORD by the prophet Isaiah:

> *no weapon forged against you will prevail,*
> *and you will refute every tongue that accuses you.*

SPIRIT OF COURAGE

This is the heritage of the servants of the LORD,
and this is their vindication from me,"
declares the LORD.

—ISAIAH 54:17

Gideon in the Old Testament book of Judges gives us some insight into how important our thinking is when it comes to battle. Gideon and his people from Manassah have some big problems. His people were in a battle only they had no leader so they had no offense. Year after year the Midianites and Amalekites would swarm over Manasseh like locusts and take or destroy everything. Most of the people would leave and in Judges chapter 6, we meet Gideon threshing wheat in a wine press. Threshing wheat means separating the grain from the shaft by beating it against a surface but usually on an elevated surface out in open air. Gideon was doing this in a wine press on the ground, a trough made of stone lined with concrete, he was hiding the wheat from the Midianites. I'm not sure Gideon had a strategy for defending his land. It seems he just had a strategy for survival. I believe that is what many of us do, we just have a strategy for survival, if I can just get through another month, week, day, hour. This is okay but it is not the abundant living that we are ordained to have as Christians.

You know, God is always calling us to live the abundant life. He speaks to us through his word and other people. He guides us in our circumstances. God has all kinds of strategies to get our attention so that we may do this thing called life his way. While Gideon was in the winepress, God sent angels to tell him that he was a mighty warrior. Gideon thought God was mistaken. He made God show him a sign before he would believe it and when God revealed himself through a sign, Gideon's faith and courage grew. Gideon had a big problem getting a hold of how God saw him. Gideon was not a mighty warrior. He didn't think so and no one he knew would describe him as a mighty warrior. So what was God talking about?

God is telling Gideon that God has plans for him to finally be the mighty warrior that God created him to be. But Gideon didn't see it or believe it. Gideon, however, did have enough faith in God to know that if this really was from God, then it was the truth. He acknowledged that the truth about all things comes from God. He also knew that the only way that he could be a mighty warrior was for it to be ordained by God. God's almighty power had to be Gideon's backup. After God was gracious enough to show Gideon three signs, three times that God was talking to him, he accepted the call.

This is one of the classic examples of a prophetic call from God. Moses, Gideon, and Jeremiah share the components of the prophetic call of God: confrontation, commission, objections, assurance, and sign. I believe God is always calling God's chosen people, whether we hear it or not. In other words, God was calling Moses, Gideon, and Jeremiah, among others before they realized. I say this because for me I can recall a lifetime of God calling me, only I didn't know that is what it was. For me I can identify three prophetic calls from God or maybe all along it was the same one calling but I needed three stages. The call to reconciling close family relationships, the call to the Gospel ministry, and then the call to get a formal seminary education. All three of these calls required courage. Not just courage, but a spirit of courage that comes from God.

The call to reconciling relationships particularly reviving my marriage had to happen first before the other two would be possible. Reconciliation requires healing, forgiveness, overcoming shame, and breaking generational curses. I had to do two things to be able to revive my marriage, study the word of God and stop drinking alcohol. These are the conditions I needed to create an atmosphere in my life built on an altar of peace that focuses on Jehovah Shalom. Jehovah Shalom is the God of peace, wholeness, and health where nothing is missing and nothing is broken. Maintaining sobriety and meditating on the word of God is a major part of my daily ritual. Maximus in the movie Gladiator whose motto was "strength and honor" had a ritual that before he engaged in a fight, he would pick up some dirt and rub his hands together. It reminded him of his farm, his wife and son. They represented peace to him and that is where he got the strength and the courage to be an undefeated warrior.

Reconciling relationships, ministering the Gospel, and attending seminary all require the same peace, strength, and courage. Every day we need to do something to remind us of our peace. We need to remember who we are and trust who we belong to because this is the foundation of our spirit of courage. Accepting the call to the Gospel ministry requires trust in God period. Attending seminary at age 44 while being a wife, mother of two and a practicing anesthesiologist required encouragement, inner peace, and joy all originating from the Holy Spirit. I believe God's goal for my tripartite calling is for me to get more intimate with God and to develop my spirit of courage to serve God for the rest of my life.

WAGING WAR

As Christians, we know that we are winners, that we can do all things through Christ who strengthens us according to his purpose, and no weapon formed against us shall prosper. This is a winning attitude. Before going into battle one must already see victory at the end of the fight.

Whenever I am trying to figure out how to handle a problem or battle, I look to see how Jesus handled it in the New Testament. Jesus had some battles to deal with. But they may not have been what you think. He did not battle against the Pharisees or Caesar Augustus. Jesus' greatest battle was against the minds of his followers. How was he going to teach the disciples to continue with the ministry after her was gone?

Typical of the times, Jesus ended his ministry with a fellowship meal. Interestingly enough at the end of the meal he washed his disciples feet again. He did this to demonstrate that the ministry had to be about the disciples serving people. Since it is most likely that their feet were washed when they entered the upper room, I believe Jesus really wanted to make an unforgettable point about how his disciples should treat each other. He told them about the peace that he was leaving them and then he told them to arise; get up and go.

In all three gospels, Jesus tells the disciples to get up and go and in Luke it's get up and pray. The point is that we must get up. We must do something. We must take the peace that Jesus left us and get up and go help someone, hug someone, feed someone, smile at someone, give to someone, lay hands on someone, pray for someone. Get up and go back to school, find a job, volunteer, clean the house, clean your room, clean the car, get up and go. Go to church, go to Sunday school, bible study, power hour, get up and go and do. These are the weapons that Jesus wants us to use to fight our battles: our belief and faith in God, the word of God, praise, worship, love, kindness, and forgiveness. These are interesting and yet unusual weapons to use to fight battles, but they are powerful and very effective. Yelling, screaming, cursing, hitting, throwing, back-biting, gossiping, negative talking, don't work. Ignoring people doesn't work either.

I used to make people invisible when they hurt me. The anger, hurt and rejection was killing me. My answer to protect myself was to make them invisible. Make them not exist. Poof! Then they could never hurt me again. I don't know where I learned this from, but I know that I learned it young. There was no forgiveness going on in my home when I was growing up. Children are victims of their parents, for better and for worse.

My mother said that she would never say I'm sorry. As a mother she was privileged never to have to say I'm sorry. At the same time she said mothers should never feel guilty. It is wasted energy. What a combination? I think only God never has to say I'm sorry and is guiltless. She would do whatever it took to take care of her kids, which included lying, cheating, and stealing.

In her defense, she was hurt and rejected by her mother. Her mother treated her like a slave since she was the eldest daughter of 13 children. She cooked, cleaned, rocked, dressed, and protected her siblings not getting any approval or appreciation from her mother. Everything blew up when her father and brother were killed when she was 16 years old. All of this loss and rejection is enough to destroy a life by destroying a person's thinking about herself, her life and others. I imagine it is like being in combat perpetually. The next year she got married and gave birth to my big brother. But she still had to maintain my grandmother's home cooking, cleaning, and caring for her siblings while keeping a separate home for her family. She eventually got her GED and 3 more kids in 4 years.

By far I had it better than my mother, but I did not learn to forgive, I learned to get revenge. Making they who hurt me invisible is an aspect of my revenge. My revenge was self-righteous, crisp and dignified. Mostly it was spiritual. My thoughts were of cursing and badness. I took every disappointment personally. Jesus didn't do that, he forgave those who condemned him to the cross just as God is forgiving us all the time. So who do I need to forgive:

1. Myself for not being perfect, being loud, eating too much, not exercising, being too emotional

2. Mommy and Pop for rejection, betrayal, lying, alcohol abuse, getting rid of my dog, Nuisance

3. Daddy for abandonment, rejection, betrayal, lacking courage to fight for me and my siblings

4. The Holmes clan for abandonment after the divorce, forgetting about me and my siblings, treating me better than my siblings as if I was better than them because I am a doctor

5. Nana for hurting my mother, not loving me, lying

6. The Manning clan for lying, sexual perversion, cheating, stealing, prostitution

7. My husband for rejection and betrayal

8 My siblings for rejection and betrayal

9 My children for disobedience

10 My boss for not being fair and verbal insults

11 My supervisors for not being fair and verbal insults

12 My professors for not being fair and verbal insults

13 My Church family for hypocrisy and hurting others

The problem is I came to a point where everybody was on my invisible list. My parents, aunts, uncles, cousins, my husband, colleagues at work, church folk, etc. Only my siblings and my children benefited from the sliver of mercy in my heart. Probably because I love them unconditionally, like I love my arm or hand or foot. I have no choice. They are not perfect, they mess up and they have hurt me. But, I never let the hurt go deep. I guess maybe because I know they love me.

I have never been really mad at my children for a long time. If they sense my rejection they almost immediately work it out with me. I raised them to settle problems between us and quickly, no grudges. I repeatedly would say to them from when they were very young, "I love you forever, no matter what," or "nothing could stop me from loving you, ever!" Our family motto is "harmony."

We have to have an attitude of peace and harmony. Even in the midst of our struggles we have to have an attitude of peace. The goal is harmony with our family, our friends, and our neighbors but most importantly harmony with God. In other words, Christ does not want us to take up arms in our battles. Our enemy is not flesh and blood but principalities, wrong thinking and wrong spirits. You fight these things with spiritual weapons such as prayer and peace.

So, with an attitude of peace and harmony Jesus Christ sent his disciples to continue the work of the ministry preaching the gospel, healing the sick, deliverance from demons, etc. in preparation of his death and resurrection.

On the evening of that our Lord and Savior Jesus Christ was resurrected, the disciples were locked up in a room scared, sad, confused, depressed. Their leader, mentor, and teacher was just brutally murdered, crucified for no good reason, now what were they going to do?

The disciples were gathered together locked up in a room. I don't know how but they came together. Without phones, texting, Facebook, or Twitter, but somehow they came together. Remember they scattered apart during the crucifixion, they went different ways, maybe that is why Thomas was not there.

But what happens to the plan or your mission when the leader dies? Does the movement die, does the mission die? For sure the leader would want things to continue. But no matter what, things do change. What happens when you lose your job, your house, your health, your car, spouse, your child, your parent? What do you do when the rug gets pulled from under you?

Have you ever been blindsided?

Christ knows that his disciples would need some major help and guidance at this low point. This would be considered a valley experience. Some may say that most of our time on earth is in the valley and that there can only be a few mountain top experiences. I don't know but I know that we can get some help from Jesus in the Gospel of John chapter 14 verse 27, *"Peace I leave with you; my peace I give you. I do not give to you as the world gives. Do not let your hearts be troubled and do not be afraid."*

Let's look at what Jesus tells them, "Peace." And he repeats it. Christ came back to his group pretty quickly after they discovered that he was resurrected, probably as soon as enough of them gathered together. He didn't waste any time. He gave them no time to come up with another strategy or plan. Whatever they may have been coming up with, he nipped it in the bud. The disciples had many options: quit, start violent riots against the Jews, riot against the Romans, split up, etc.

As my mother would say, they had to regroup. Jesus' appearance here resets the disciples in the spirit of courage. They are to believe in the resurrection, that's why he showed them his scars and wounds. They are to have an attitude of peace. They are to go out and continue the ministry. And they are to receive the Holy Spirit. Jesus did an amazing thing here. He breathed on them for forgiveness. The message is that forgiveness is life-giving like breathing. Let us consider that Jesus wants us to wage war in the spirit of courage through forgiveness.

Lessons Learned

1. These are the weapons that Jesus wants us to use to fight our battles: our belief and faith in God, the word of God, praise, worship, love, kindness, and forgiveness.

2. Weapons of spiritual warfare are service and peace.

3. Be peace and breathe forgiveness. Its important.

SIX

Courage in the Face of Friendly Rejection

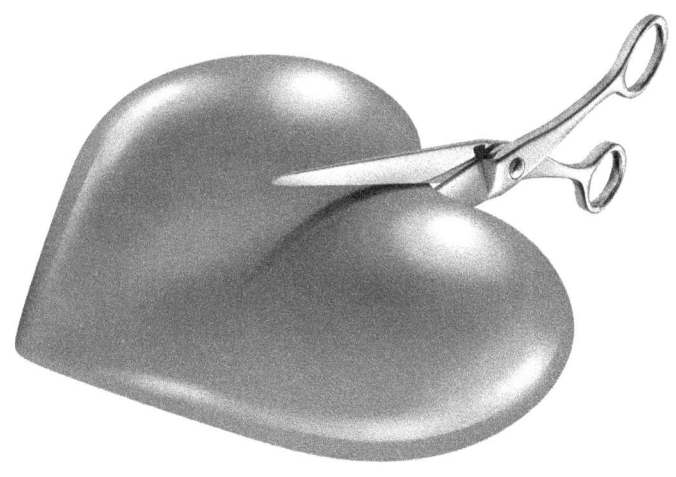

I've always had the feeling of protection surrounding me, that I was special. This Easter Sunday, my big brother confirmed it for me. We were sitting at my Mother's kitchen table and he said, "Ever since you were a little girl, I knew there was something different, special about you. There is a cloud around you. Not a bad cloud. A shining light all around you."

Even with all this light emanating from me, I never had a lot of friends. The friendships I did have, they didn't last long. My first true friends were pets. I fell in love with our family pets. I think I clung too much to them. I was looking for love and they gave it. The problem was that they all died! I am 49 years old and I still cry when I think about my childhood pets. I cry over them way more than I do over both my grandmothers. They lived with me. They loved me. They slept with me. They ran to me whenever I came home from school. But somehow I haven't gotten over the loss.

I picked up my son from football practice and we were driving down a busy road, Middle Country Road, in Coram, New York, and all of a sudden we see this very small brown dog cross the street. I slowed down and swerved a little to avoid hitting the dog; one hand on the wheel the other over my mouth. Then I had flashbacks. I remembered, husband Eric telling me never to avoid animals in the road because I could get in an accident with another car. I remembered the white puppy that Pop ran over in our driveway when I was around 10 years old. Then I started to cry. My son said, "Come on Ma you're not going to cry?" I didn't say anything, trying to hold back the tears but that usually doesn't work for me. He said, "Man up Ma!" The tears kept flowing and I said to him, "That's why you can't have a dog." There is no way that I could allow myself or my kids to be hurt from the loss of pets.

But, why did I hurt so much? Why does it still affect me? When I was in seminary it came up and I cried during class. That was four years ago. I knew then that I needed therapy. I told the class about Nuisance, a basset hound. She was an orangish-brown and black "hot dog" dog. I loved her and she loved me. I was around 10 years old and she slept with me. I was the only one in the family that truly loved her. She had a behavior problem and she was not "potty trained." Every day she urinated or left feces on the carpet and one of us children had to clean it up. My brothers especially hated her and they beat her. One day I came home from school and Nuisance was gone. I looked everywhere for her. I screamed, "Nuisance, Nuisance, Nusiance!" I finally gave up after several months. But it still hurts me to think about it.

To this day I believe that my mother and my step-father, took Nuisance for "a ride" and dropped her off somewhere too far away to find her way back home. They deny it but I don't believe them. I was the only one in the family that grieved over Nuisance. I was so lonely without her and I began looking for love in all the wrong places. Every place I looked, there were problems. Now I know that God is the greatest lover of me. God calls me God's friend.

I never had a whole lot of friends, it's almost as if God always wanted me just for himself. For most of my life I looked for friends and tried to fit in with groups or just people. I tried to get people to like me, want to be with me, and to love me. My high school friends were not really friends. They would let me hang around them as long as I let them ridicule and tease me. They teased me for being fat, because of the way I dressed, the way I talked, because I was smart, because I never got in trouble, because I didn't go to parties, because I always tried to do the right thing, etc. Eventually, I developed enough courage to speak up for myself and demand that they respect me. That ended the relationships. It's interesting that now as adults, these same people want to be my friends, keep in touch with me, and network with me but I don't trust them, nor do I need them to be my friends, now I minister to them.

Since college there have been more friends but I guess nothing lasts forever. I call them seasonal friendships. Especially on my journey with the Lord, friends would come to me help me grow in Christ and then go. I kept growing in Christ but their growth always hit a plateau. They would only go so far with me and then the rejection came. They would stop journeying with me, stop interacting with me, it was over.

First there was Lynda. She was in her 30s and I was 16. I met her at Brookhaven National Laboratory and she went to my church. She also hung out with my boyfriend's mother and his aunt. He was in Atlanta and I kept busy going to church and hanging out with Lynda. Because of these interactions, I got saved when I was seventeen. I was baptized on March 1, 1981, my boyfriend's birthday. I went to Atlanta the day after I graduated from high school to be in a summer science program at Spelman College and be with Eric. Lynda moved to Virginia the next year. That season was over.

Then there was Carla. She was a single mother. Her mother-in-law was a Baptist minister. We interacted in church, her daughters were friends with Amanda. We visited each other's home. She went on Women's Retreat and we shared a room together. We discussed our husbands and their infidelities. We shared confidences. Then I found out that she really was not married. He really was married to someone else. Once she told me the truth, the decline began and the season was over.

Then there was Jill. She lived down the street from me. She was really into prayer and bible study. She and her husband were Lay ministers in the Methodist church. Now they were ministers in our church. I was not a minister yet. I just loved God and learning about God and the bible. We would visit one another, their son Jack who was older than my kids would play together. Jill started a phone prayer group with Melissa, Dawn, me, and Jill's sister. Every morning at 5:30 we would call one another on conference call, read scripture and pray. We read through the whole bible in almost 2 years. First Dawn dropped out. Then Jill's sister dropped out. Then Melissa dropped out. Then it was just me and Jill. Then Jill got offended by something I said. I probably told her the truth about something that she did not want to hear.

Probably she thought I judged her. I've been known to offend people with my love for the truth.

Of all the people, I knew my friendship with Melissa would last forever. But now the season is over. The only friendship that truly lasts forever is with Jesus Christ. My sister Val has been trying to tell me for years that Melissa and I are not on the same journey. Today I realize that discipline on this Christian journey makes a difference. Someone may say that they are on the journey with me, they may want to be, but if their focus is not following Christ, no matter how hard the assignment, then we are really going in two different directions.

When I made a chart of our endeavors on paper, I realized that we have been on two different tracts. I expected Melissa to have the spiritual results I was having even though she was not doing what I was doing to grow spiritually like finishing school of religion training and continuing in ministry.

I have finally stopped assuming that people are my friends. God has called me to give up that mission because He has called me His friend. Not that God is my friend, but God says that I am his friend. There's a difference. Abraham believed and obeyed God. He possessed the righteousness of God. He was in harmony with God and God called him friend. God's friend Abraham walked with God step by step.

I learned this from a song called, "I am a Friend of God," by Israel Houghton while at an anesthesiology conference with my husband in Hawaii in 2005. It was a combination trip of business and celebrating our 20th wedding anniversary. Some songs deserve our attention, our meditation, our singing out loud to the top of our lungs. I purchased the CD because it contained a song that we danced to in our dance ministry. I bought it on the trip with me because I love listening to praise and worship songs. They help keep me focused on God. The first song on the 2nd CD is "I am a Friend of God." We were staying in the Hilton hotel in Waikiki Beach, Honolulu high up with an ocean view. I was on the balcony singing out loud to the roaring Pacific ocean. "I am a friend of God." I was in heaven. A year and a half later I accepted the called to the Gospel Ministry. I didn't know what I was doing but God called me friend. What I was looking for in a friend, was too much to ask from any human being. I wanted everything; complete and total love, forgiveness, and undivided attention. No human being was able to be that for me. Now I know that God wanted me exclusively for himself and I surrender to God. I surrender my unrealistically high expectations of people to Christ.

There is a lot of grief in this Christian walk. We have wonderful interactions and relationships, but they don't last forever. The only relationship that lasts forever is with God. When there is a death, there must be a grieving process. Break ups are painful but necessary if we are going to continue to grow. I learned that my expectations for each of these women was not theirs. To this day I don't even know what their expectations were. I believe I became too much for them. Too intimidating. I wonder if they saw the cloud of shining light that my brother could see all around me and it was too much to handle. Who wants to be around God all the time? Meeeeeeeee! Oh, well too bad for them.

In therapy with Miss Nelly, I learned to speak the truth in love to people and don't look back. Don't look back meaning it is God's job to work in, with and through people. I am just the messenger speaking God's words. I'm planting the seeds of God's word and God does the watering and provides the sun. But God also gives us free will to choose to want to listen to and understand God's messages, or not. Unfortunately some people may not truly be able to understand what God is saying and doing because of the barriers they place before God. The major barrier of having different agendas from God's will.

Jesus' disciples did not understand their master basically because their mission was opposite of Jesus' mission. Jesus came to teach love and forgiveness, to heal bodies and souls, to be brutally crucified, to die, and to be resurrected. They wanted Jesus to start a revolution and take over the leadership of Israel. No way did they expect Jesus to die. They could not even bare to see him arrested and crucified. They abandoned him and rejected him. This is what friends do too when they are not on the same page, not being in one accord. The problem is that many times we think we are on one accord but we aren't. There is deception lurking in a lot of friendships. But it all comes out in the wash. Don't think that you and your friends are better than Jesus and his friends.

The same thing at work. You think you have friends at work. You eat lunch together, sit next to each other at meetings, exchange Christmas gifts, discuss each other's children and husbands, etc. Then one day they disagree with you or don't back you up in a meeting. They make disparaging remarks about you in public. They take credit for the work you did. It is obvious that they are not truly happy for your successes. They are really not your friends. The best friend I have is God. God called me God's friend. So, I wonder who is going to be my next seasonal friend. Actually, I am excited about it.

Lessons Learned

1. There is no better friend than Jesus.
2. Don't be surprised if your friendships don't last forever.
3. The promises of God are forever.
4. Protect your relationship with God with boundaries around everything else.

SEVEN

Worship instead of Worry

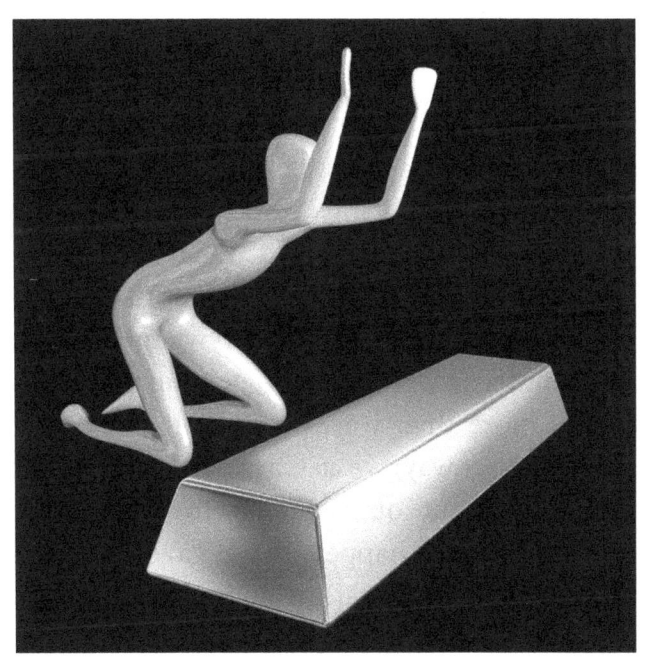

SPIRIT OF COURAGE

> *"Therefore I tell you, do not worry about your life, what you will eat or drink; or about your body, what you will wear. Is not life more than food, and the body more than clothes?"*
>
> —Matthew 6:25

Life in 2013 is complicated. The virtue of simplicity has been lost to the global world of instant gratification, fast food, and social media. Our modern culture makes traditional church worship services boring and seemingly a waste of time. Some liturgies are more entertaining than others but the purpose of liturgies is worship and not entertainment. I remind us that that we were created by God to worship God. If one were to read the bible cover to cover, one would understand that the main theme is that humans were created to worship the one true living God of the bible, the God of Abraham, Isaac, and Jacob.

I propose that another way of looking at how we live our lives is to consider striving to worship God in everything we do and not just on Sunday. Therefore the idea that some liturgies don't feel like worship is absurd because worship is not a feeling. Since God is with us always and is everywhere at the same time maybe we should worry more about worshipping God in all our circumstances more than we worry about the circumstances. Let me say it another way; we as Christians don't spend enough time wondering about our worship to God, individual or collective. What would happen if we gave up just worrying about one problem or situation and instead worried about worshipping, praising and praying to God.

What is worship? Worship is an action. Worship is something that is done. It is actively connecting with God. Worship is submitting to the one who is always with us. It is getting intimate with God through relationship. Worship is based on the belief that God is worthy of our attempts to worship. Our attempts to worship God are our way of communicating to God God's high value. Worship is acknowledging God's superiority over us humans this is why we bow down in the presence of God. We are saying "God I understand You are greater than me. You have the answers for my life, I bow down to Your authority." Worship is the respect that we give to God that is based on gratitude for God being our God.

God so loved the world that he gave his only begotten son that whosoever shall believe in him shall not perish but have ever lasting life. (John 3:16) Worship is showing respect out of a sense of gratitude to the one who gave everything to reconcile us to our Redeemer. It is more than just a Sunday experience. To worship properly entails giving our entire lives over to God's purpose. In our talk, our walk, play, and work. Every aspect of our lives should be given over to honoring, submitting and respecting God.

Some of the things that are done in worship are: falling on one's face, being humble before God, confessing, surrendering, honesty, rejoicing, and resting in God. The most important aspect of worshipping God is God. It's not about any one of us, it is only about God. And by *it* I mean everything. Everything is about God.

> *In the beginning God created the heavens and the earth. Now the earth was formless and empty, darkness was over the surface of the deep, and the Spirit of God was hovering over the waters. And God said, "Let there*

> *be light," and there was light. God saw that the light was good, and he separated the light from the darkness. God called the light "day," and the darkness he called "night." And there was evening, and there was morning—the first day.*
>
> —Genesis 1:1-5

The ever-expanding, hovering God created everything before the beginning. God is a Spirit and hovers over everything that we could ever imagine exists. This is the reason why we worship God. We must worship God with integrity because God is worthy of our worship.

The purpose of worshipping God is to glorify God and the reason we were created. God loves us so much that God gives us new mercies every day. Remember that Hezekiah told God that if he were dead, he would not be able to praise and worship God, so God added 15 years to his life.(2 Kings 20:6, Isaiah 38:5) God requires that we be God's workers on earth. We are to follow after God's agenda and be God's apprentices. We are to have the Almighty's purposes in mind and learn our skills from God. To this endeavor God gave us scripture. God is gracious to provide all that we need to do God's work with skill and cunning. "Do your best to present yourself to God as one approved, a workman who does not need to be ashamed and who correctly handles the word of truth." (2 Tim 2:15) God's servants must live and work to honor and worship the Lord our God and serve Him only.

Worship is not a spectator sport. It is done by individuals alone or in groups. The people of God gather together to participate in worship through singing to the LORD from the heart, listening to the preached word of God, meditating on the word of God, praying to God, and giving to build up God's kingdom. "Therefore, I urge you, brothers and sisters, in view of God's mercy, to offer your bodies as a living sacrifice, holy and pleasing to God—this is your true and proper worship." (Romans 12:1)

The circumstances of life get easier to deal with when we surrender our lives to God. I believe that we will be extra blessed when we choose to worship God instead of worry about stuff. Yes, stuff is real, stuff is bad, stuff is hard, stuff is trying to destroy you, but God is with us and God knows all about it. Most importantly, God is almighty and is able to deliver us from all of this stuff. This is where we get our courage.

The spirit of courage means that you keep going even though you are living under a threat. How? Keep studying the word of God, prayer, meditation and praise. The apostle Paul had a way of living under the threat of death and danger throughout his ministry. He was safe and sound until he had an encounter with Christ. After that he was always living in danger because he chose to follow Christ. Not only did he follow Christ, he was bold about it. He journeyed throughout Asia Minor preaching and teaching the Gospel message. In the face of danger and persecution, he went back to Jerusalem knowing that there was a good chance that he would be arrested, and he was. Nonetheless, he went and he preached and he was arrested. He declared his Roman citizenship and bought himself a ticket to Rome. It took three ships to get him to Rome, one Asian ship and two Alexandrian granary ships. On the way to Rome there was a shipwreck, a poisonous snake bite and more while Paul was shackled to Julius, his Roman Praetorian centurion guard.

Imagine this unique couple. Paul and his guard, shackled together. Paul was probably loquacious and the guard was probably quiet. Paul probably said, "Thank you Lord Jesus," like my sister Valerie says all the time. He was probably praying in psalms, singing praises to God and worshipping God daily, routinely. They started the journey on a ship from Adramyttium along the coast of Asia. I wonder what Julius thought of Paul? Whatever Julius was thinking we know he had a merciful heart towards Paul. "The next day we landed at Sidon; and Julius, in kindness to Paul, allowed him to go to his friends so they might provide for his needs." (Acts 27:3) I suppose Julius was not satisfied with the way this Asian ship handled in difficult weather because when they got to Myra in Lycia he switched them to an Alexandrian granary ship heading to Italy.

This granary ship ran into trouble too and Paul warned the centurion, the soldiers, and the crew of the pending disaster and great loss to the ship and cargo and loss of life if they sail from Crete. They did not listen. During the storm Paul told them to keep their courage and stay on the ship and no one will die. "Last night an angel of the God whose I am and whom I serve stood beside me and said, 'Do not be afraid, Paul. You must stand trial before Caesar, and God has graciously given you the lives of all who sail with you.'" (Acts 27:23-24) Paul was telling them to have courage, while he was having courage himself. It's hard to keep something we know about and have personal experience with to ourselves, especially when we are in a bad situation and we know how to get through it. "So keep up your courage, men, for I have faith in God that it will happen just as he told me. Nevertheless, we must run aground on some island." (vv25-26)

Paul had faith, he demonstrated it, he spoke it and he taught it. Because of the power of the author of his faith, he had courage, he spoke it and he taught it. Julius witnessed all of this. He most likely even heard Paul speaking in tongues since we know that he spoke in tongues frequently.(1 Cor 14:18) Speaking in tongues is worship. It is communication with God in our spiritual language.

I thank God that when I don't know what to pray for anymore, I can pray in tongues! For sure, I have prayed for my son more than any other individual. I have smeared him with anointing oil more than any other. I have laid my hands on his head more than any other person. When we were in that trial, what else could I say to God that I have not already said? So, I prayed in tongues. I continued to "schmear" him with oil, I still laid hands on him, but now I could just pray in the spirit knowing that my spirit is praying to God. What comfort I receive from praying in tongues.

During this waiting for my son's name to be cleared, I refused to speak about the situation unless it was absolutely necessary to my husband and to my lawyers and to my therapist. There was no idle talk. There was no talk laced with fear. I remained triumphant. I knew that God was going to vindicate my son, because God promised, actually in several places in the bible, especially in the Old Testament. You have to know the bible for yourself so you can have the courage to believe what God says about your situation.

"The LORD will vindicate his people and relent concerning his servants when he sees their strength is gone and no one is left, slave or free."

—Deut 32:36

"I cry out to God Most High, to God, who vindicates me."

—Psalms 57:2

"'The LORD has vindicated us; come, let us tell in Zion what the LORD our God has done."

—Jer 51:10

Worry never helps. In fact, worry can actually make things worse. How many times have we impulsively done things out of fear and worry that only made the situation even worse? How many times have we shared struggles and difficulties with so-called friends and family members only to get horrible advice or they use it against you or they spread it to the world? One really good rule to live by is don't tell someone your problems unless you are sure they can help you solve it. I mean truly solve the problem not just emotionally make you feel better. Trust God and let the Holy Spirit make you feel better. God knows all the details and knows the truth. Your friend doesn't know all the details or the truth. God has all wisdom, your friend may not be wise at all. In fact, your friend is more inclined to tell you lies to try to make you feel better because a lot of times the truth hurts. We may even believe our friendship is in jeopardy if we actually say what we think is the truth. We never have to doubt God's friendship.

WORSHIP INSTEAD OF WORRY

All my life I have been looking for friends, trying to fit in with people, and trying to get people to like me, want to be with me, and to love me. I have finally given up on that mission. God has called me to give up that mission because, like Abraham, God has called me friend.

> *Our God, did you not drive out the inhabitants of this land before your people Israel and give it forever to the descendants of Abraham your friend?*
>
> —2 Chronicles 20:7

> *"But you, Israel, my servant, Jacob, whom I have chosen, you descendants of Abraham my friend,"*
>
> —Isaiah 41:8

> *And the scripture was fulfilled that says, "Abraham believed God, and it was credited to him as righteousness," and he was called God's friend.*
>
> —James 2:23

> *I no longer call you servants, because a servant does not know his master's business. Instead, I have called you friends, for everything that I learned from my Father I have made known to you.*
>
> —John 15:15

Abraham believed and obeyed God, therefore, he possessed the righteousness of God. Abraham was in harmony with God and God called him friend. He walked with God step by step. Because of the blood Jesus shed on the cross for my sins I am a descendant of Abraham and a friend of God. Not that God is my friend, but God says that I am God's friend. There's a difference. God chooses me as God's friend because of Christ. Since God calls me God's friend, why would I ever have to worry about anything?

Lessons Learned

1. Worry never solved one problem.

2. Have faith and worship God.

3. Seek God first then everything else will come.

4. Be patient and wait on God.

5. Don't do things out of desperation except pray, praise, and worship God.

6. You really only have control over yourself and your minor children.

EIGHT

Desperate Prayer

As I look back over my live I realize that I have a habit of taking advantage of opportunities. Somehow I knew that I was blessed, gifted, and highly favored from a young age but I also knew that people, situations, and institutions were against me because I was a black women from Gordon Heights, a black neighborhood in Long Island, New York. My parents taught me and my sisters and brothers to take care of ourselves, do the right thing, make our own way, get help from wherever we could. To take advantage of situations. I interpreted that to mean that I needed to find ways to make people, systems, institutions, schools, see how special I was, because I knew I was. A black woman with no important connections and no money needed something extra. So the things I did were Girl Scouts, volunteering for the American Cancer Society, the Leukemia Society of America, the local drill team, Knights of the Purple Haze, Brookhaven National Lab Medical Department, etc. But even doing these things may not have given me the advantage I needed if I was not an excellent student.

The important thing about being an excellent student is not the grades, but the character that goes along with getting the grades. In other words when people notice you doing the best you can and putting forth honest effort, they will be willing to do the same and put forth honest effort on your behalf. This effort from others to help, assist, and intercede is leverage. I love this word. It means advantage to lift up. Leverage raises you to a higher level that normally would not be attainable without this advantage. In Spanish it is levanter, it reminds us of the word levitate.

What is leverage? Leverage is edge, favor, and advantage. Do you have any leverage?

When Michael Steele served as the *first African-American* chairman of the *Republican National Committee* from January 2009 until January 2011 I got hopeful that Black people had a voice in the Republican party. I was wrong. He is Black but his policies aren't. President Barack Obama is serving his second term as the first Black president of the United States. Surely, Black people have some leverage in the White House, but Congress is making sure that it is not as much as we hoped.

In the old Testament book of Numbers chapter 14, Moses is leading the Israelites to the land of milk and honey after they were delivered from several plagues and from bondage. Moses was leading them into freedom. They crossed the red sea on dry land and watched the Pharaoh's army drown. You might say that Moses provided leverage for the people. I do believe that the job of leaders is to provide leverage for the people they lead. Yes, hopefully, leaders bring edge, advantage, and favor to their people. Leverage through courage, vision, strength and love.

Clearly, Moses loved the Israelites. They loved him too, but they had some issues. Sometimes the people we are in charge of lose the vision, get scared, get discouraged and lose faith and they want to go back to the way it used to be. Imagine, if Black people in America can't take having both democratic and republican party leaders be black men? I can't imagine it at all, and maybe Moses couldn't imagine what he heard from his people, that they wanted to go back to Egypt! Back to Egypt! Are they crazy? Have you ever been there before? Have you ever tried to help people? Try to give them an advantage? Help get them out of a big mess, only to hear them curse you and wish that you never helped them in the first place. What do you do? Do you curse back at them? Tell them off, write them off, abandon them, leave them, or sell them to someone else. Do you leave them? Do you start to hate them? What did Moses and Aaron do? The fell on their faces, they got on the ground, they got in their serious prayer stance. Stance is a position of leverage, readiness, advantage and edge to begin to fight. Moses and Aaron knew only God could help them with this situation and they needed help now. I am so impressed with Moses and Aaron. They just fell to the ground, face down, humble and prostrate before the Lord. That was their war stance. The Lord spoke to Moses. He got a word from the Lord and not only that, Moses was able to plea for the people's lives. God was going to wipe them all out and raise up for Moses and Aaron a new nation. God was really, really, angry with the people. Please don't ever take God for granted and think that God does not get angry with our disobedience, ungratefulness, and lack of faith. I just wonder, where does your leverage come from? Does it come from our leaders, having money, property, knowing important people, or does it come from God.

Moses and Aaron were serious leverage for the people because they had the courage to go before God on their behalf, even though they didn't deserve it. This is what Jesus does for us now. Jesus intercedes to God for those who believe in him. This leverage came from God. I believe our ultimate leverage is comes from knowing, loving, trusting, and obeying God. Sure we would have more leverage in politics if President Obama was our friend, more leverage in business if we had billions of dollars in cash, or more leverage in ….whatever. Don't be fooled. You need to know that your leverage, leverage for your finances, leverage for your kids, your husband, your grades, your health comes from God, it comes from the wonderful, matchless love of God. God loves you. *Hesed*, one of my favorite biblical Hebrew words, means lovingkindness. God cannot stop loving us with this special kind of love that lasts forever. This is where your leverage is.

Because of the leverage I have through my relationship with Christ, God answers all of my prayers. Not because I am so good. Not because I am so holy. Just because of Jesus and because God promised. My spirit is seated in heavenly places with Christ. My body and soul are being renewed and transformed every single day. But my spirit is right with God. My spirit agrees with God. My spirit agrees with the word of God and the promises of God. Therefore, when I pray, God always hears and answers. Not only that, but the scripture says that Jesus prays for me to the Father. I must be blessed because Jesus prays for me. Not just for me but for anybody and

DESPERATE PRAYER

everybody that believes that Jesus is the son of God and died on the cross for his or her sins and was resurrected on the third day with all power in his hands. God is no respecter of persons.

I know that I am God's favorite. I know that with every part of my being and I pray that you know that too for yourself. God is awesome enough for each person who believes to claim that she is God's favorite. Because God loves me so much and I am God's favorite, I have confidence in my prayers. My spirit of courage comes from this confidence I have in the love that resulted in Christ dying for me. So when all hell is breaking loose, I pray to God in faith.

I pray more to have less control I have over circumstances. As I grow in Christ, one consistent thing I have noticed is that God is interested in me depending totally on God. Nothing else but God. Not my intellect, not my clout, not my academic titles, not my degrees, not how smart I am, not how good I memorize, nothing but God.

God is funny. I got saved the spring before I went to college. At that time, I prayed a lot for my grades but my desperate prayers were for my family. I was always an excellent student and I loved to study and get A's, so my prayers before tests were truly secondary to my outstanding study habits. Prayers for my family who were a thousand miles away were primary. I had no other option. They were not prayers to fall back on, they were all I had. I thank God for honoring my prayers and watching over my family when I was in college, especially my sister and my nephew. My sister is totally, absolutely, and joyfully on fire for the LORD. She is director of the dance ministry at my church and every time she ministers the dance with her

"Dancing Angels," glory hallelujah! There are no words to describe how in awe of God I am. God deserves all the glory, honor and praise! Prayer in faith works.

Prayer is one very important major tool required to have and maintain the spirit of courage. The older I get, the more desperate my prayers become. Many people know about the benefits of prayer, but it must be as vital as breathing is to life. I've learned, however, that for me, praying in English is not always enough. I learned this when my son was falsely accused, suspended from school, and the object of a police investigation. My son who was practically born in church, goes to Sunday School every Sunday, played the drums for church since he was 7 years old, and now at 15 plays the piano too. My son who is big and strong physically but gentle and kind spiritually was taught by me since he was able to walk to be a gentleman. I used to tell him when he was a little boy "make it soft" around little girls to remind him to not to hurt them, even if accidently. Since he was a baby, I have prayed over my son on a greater magnitude than my daughter because he is a Black male. The plight of Black males in the US is less than optimal. When he became a teenager, I routinely laid hands on his head and frequently anointed his head with oil. I guess what I am saying is that I did everything I knew to do to protect my son.

The only new thing that I hadn't done before to fight for my son was praying in tongues. I had already prayed all I knew to pray in English. What else could I say? What else could I ask for? Praying in tongues was so comforting because I knew that my spirit was praying to the spirit of God in a most powerful way that I could not understand.

Speaking in tongues has not been addressed in a significant way in my religious upbringing until recently. Baptist people seem to have a problem with speaking in tongues and I'm not sure why other than ignorance. Paul said plainly, that he spoke in tongues more than the people he taught and preached to. (1 Cor 14:18) Clearly speaking in tongues was not more than loving one's neighbor, but it was something to be done often and taken seriously. When you look at Paul's ministry, he needed major help. Supernatural help. Praying in tongues gave him the leverage he needed to complete the dangerous mission God gave him.

Now more than ever we must not forget that we are spiritual beings. We must feed our spirits regularly just as we feed our bodies regularly. Spiritual food is much more effective than alcohol, cigarettes, marijuana, cocaine, heroin, Ecstasy, Prozac, etc. I'm sure his centurion guard, Julius, heard Paul praying in tongues. I believe the Holy Spirit worked on Paul to have courage and on Julius to have mercy on Paul.

Lessons Learned and Reflection Questions

1. Prayer works because God answers all of our prayers according to God's will, not ours.

2. Christ is the ultimate leverage.

3. Do you have leverage?

NINE

Universal Precautions and Hospitality

I started medical school in 1985. It was a time when HIV had been around for several years and in 1987, when I was a 3rd year medical student and started taking care of patients at Boston City Hospital, the Centers for Disease Control or the CDC came up with a policy of Universal Precautions. *Universal precautions* are the infection control techniques that were recommended following the AIDS outbreak in the 1980s. Essentially it means that every patient is treated as if they are infected and therefore precautions are taken to minimize risk. Essentially, universal precautions are good hygiene habits, such as hand washing and the use of gloves and other barriers, correct sharps handling, and aseptic techniques. These precautions stress that all patients should be assumed to be infectious for blood-borne diseases such as AIDS and hepatitis B. This means that every time I go to work at Stony Brook

Medical Center, I assume that each of my patients has HIV/AIDS.

The idea is that since we cannot tell what disease a patient has just by looking at them we should assume that he or she has a communicable disease, protect ourselves and protect other patients. This will also protect the patient from any disease that the medical practitioner may have as well. So, just because a person looks cute, has fashionable clothes, speaks proper English, smells nice, drives a nice car, has several degrees, has a great job, is very old, or very young, or goes to church every Sunday, you still have to follow universal precautions.

Today, there is an HIV/AIDS pandemic and crisis in the Black community. It is the leading cause of death for black and brown women aged 25–34 years. As an ordained Baptist minister and physician, I want to use my spirit of courage and transfer this policy of Universal Precautions to the church. You can't look at a person and make a determination about her soul or what she believes. You can't look at a person and tell if she engages in a lifestyle of sin. And as a minister or parishioner, sometimes you can't even look at a person and tell if they are sick. So what does this mean?

The truth of the matter is that one could have all sorts of diseases and no one, not even a doctor, could look at a person and tell. And, in medicine, it is important to deal with the truth. Just because you don't want to believe that a person has a disease or condition, doesn't mean that they don't have it. There is not much room in excellent medical care in the 21st century for denial or pretending; denial or pretending on the part of the patient or the physician.

UNIVERSAL PRECAUTIONS AND HOSPITALITY

Following universal precautions allow people who care for sick people the freedom and the courage to provide universal hospitality. It removes anxiety and fear if we treat everybody the same. It allows us to love and care for our neighbor. Our neighbor is every human being. Everybody has the potential to have contagious diseases therefore, if we take the same precautions with everybody, we don't have to exclude anybody, or be afraid to take care of any particular person with a disease because we know that everybody we take care of could have the same disease. In other words, we don't have to guess about people and their conditions, we just have to use universal precautions and take care of everybody the same way.

Hospitals have the reputation for being places to take people who are sick. In the book of Luke, the Samaritan took the badly beaten victim of robbery to a place of hospitality, a guest house for the needy, a modern day hospital. I believe, that churches should also be places of hospitality. Churches should be places of universal hospitality. Everybody needs Jesus. Churches should have reputations for being the place to be for sick people, needy people, and especially people with HIV/AIDS. After all, isn't this the place where God is? The Holy Spirit is here right now. Everybody needs to be able to come to the house of the lord to find Jesus. Whether saved or sinner, healthy or sick, up or down, young or old, sober or intoxicated, gay or straight, male or female or other.

Let me break this down. There is no human being on the planet that should feel unwelcome in the house of the Lord. God is here, right? At no time should any human being with any condition at all, especially HIV/AIDS, believe that they were not welcome where the Holy Spirit is welcome. This means people who are homosexuals should be able to feel just as welcome in this house as the married couples or engaged men and women. People who are alcoholics or drug addicts should feel as welcome as the saved people hooked on sleeping pills, anxiety pills, pain pills, or no pills. What's the difference?

There is no condition or situation, sickness or disease that is more pure or more valid. If you are not a doctor or a scientist, why do you care how a person got the disease or the problem? What difference does it make? Don't act like it couldn't have happened to you!

The reputation of the Christian Church has got to change. People need to think that the goodness of God resides in the Christian Church. The apostle Paul told the followers of Jesus in Rome to build a loving community with people who are in need. Practice hospitality with everybody. This sanctuary has got to be a safe place for all people with all problems, those who are sanctified and those engaging in all types of sin. We say all the time don't wait to get cleaned up to come to Jesus, just come as you are. But do we really mean it? Every Easter holiday we are reminded about the Resurrection Power of Jesus Christ. As a Church, what are we doing with our Resurrection Power?

We love our churches. We each think that our church is the best that ever existed. But, I know we can do better. I know there are hurting people in all churches and all the communities. Do they know that they can come here and be fully welcome with all of their baggage, especially those with HIV/AIDS? There are sisters and brothers dying in their spirits because they have secrets. They think if we knew everything

UNIVERSAL PRECAUTIONS AND HOSPITALITY

about them, we wouldn't accept them, welcome them or love them anymore. The people of God must prove them wrong.

What are we doing with our Resurrection Power? We need to implement a policy of *Universal Hospitality and Universal Love*. We have got to show the world that God's people, the people who confess Christ, the people who harbor Resurrection Power not only say they love everybody, but show it. Let's call it a GLOBAL POLICY OF HOSPITALTIY!

So what am I saying, THERE IS NO HUMAN CONDITION THAT JESUS CANT MINISTER TO AND RESTORE. Therefore, all human-beings, along with their baggage of sin, sickness, disease, depression, fear, anxiety, personality disorders, poverty and ignorance are truly welcome in God's House. We could be fellowshipping with angels and not even know it.

This means that we openly welcome people who have HIV/AIDS. According to the Center for Disease Control's recent statistics:

- African Americans are the racial/ethnic group most affected by HIV.
- In 2009, African Americans comprised 14% of the US population but accounted for 44% of all new HIV infections.
- In 2009, black women accounted for 30% of the estimated new HIV infections among all blacks. Most (85%) black women with HIV acquired HIV through heterosexual sex. The estimated rate of new HIV infections for black women was more than 15 times as high as the rate for white women, and more than three times as high as that of Latina women.

- At some point in their lifetimes, an estimated 1 in 16 black men and 1 in 32 black women will be diagnosed with HIV infection. *http://www.cdc.gov/hiv/topics/aa/index.htm*

In other words we all have people with HIV/AIDS living among all of us. We have to come to this reality and accept it. There are many of us who have HIV and don't know it because we won't be tested. We now or in the past have engaged in high risk activities but for some reason, we won't get tested. Somehow if we don't get tested, we think we won't have the disease. This is magical thinking that results in African Americans dying of HIV/AIDS more than any other group.

Let's get together as a whole church and change our thinking about HIV as a community. Let's get rid of the stigma. We have a wonderful PEACE ministry lead by Rev Martin, but I am asking for the whole church to use the power of the Resurrection of Jesus Christ to welcome specifically people with HIV/AIDS to this church and all functions and ministries. If you are afraid, don't be. Keep focusing on the fact that the Resurrection Power is the same power that raised Jesus from the dead. If you really have that kind of power in you, what are you afraid of?

Besides, the truth of the matter is that you may already be in relationship with people with HIV/AIDS and don't even know it. As a matter of fact, I know you are. Why is this so important? Because the stigma, discrimination and secrecy of HIV/AIDS keep people from getting tested, keeps people with the disease from treatment and counseling. This means our people, the people we claim to love with the love of Jesus, are dying because of deception. They are dying inside and out because persons with HIV/AIDS are forced "outside the camp," whether it be with regard to housing, employment, insurance, school or even the practice of their religious beliefs.

The truth heals; secrets and deception kills and destroys. Let's work together to make sure the body of Christ, the church, is a church with a reputation of being a safe place for people who have HIV/AIDS, whether saved or not, where we actively practice *Universal Hospitality*.

Ana Maria Pineda said, "To welcome the stranger is to acknowledge him as a human being made in God's image; it is to treat her as one of equal worth with ourselves - indeed, as one who may teach us something out of the richness of experiences different from our own."

Lessons Learned

1. Go global with Jesus.
2. God so loved the world.
3. Do no harm. Don't hurt God's people.
4. Focus on God and not other people's short-comings.
5. Sin is sin. Gossip is just as ugly to God as sexual immorality. Don't fool yourself.

TEN

Keep Moving Forward

I am strong and courageous. I am not afraid. I am not discouraged for the LORD my God will be with me wherever I go.

—Joshua 1:9

Moving forward was the theme of President Barack Obama's re-election campaign. Forward direction is also a continuing theme in the bible. It makes sense to keep moving forward throughout life. Focusing on the past is stifling and destructive. Ignoring the lessons of the past is foolish, however learning from the past is wisdom. Obsession with the past will undoubtedly result in losing present blessings to be alive into the future. We are called to always invest in the missions for the future.

Two of the most important missions for the future in the bible were given to Joshua and of course, Jesus. Joshua was Moses' protégé. He was chosen by God to lead the people of Israel to the promise land after Moses died. God told Joshua to have courage and to focus on the word of God. Joshua was chosen because he was a faithful and loyal warrior for God. Joshua was sure of God's presence and power in his life. He was sure that God would do what God promised God would do. Joshua had complete, 100%, total confidence in the power of God, the love of God, and the will of God.

I would choose Joshua to be the most courageous servant of God. Technically he was commanded to be what God already created him to be, strong and courageous. Joshua is one of my favorite people in the bible. He demonstrated amazing human character. He was Moses' faithful assistant. He was a brave soldier. He loved God. He needed encouragement from God to lead difficult, faithless, stiff-necked people to the Promise Land. He never needed encouragement to fight in battles of war and risk his life for the sake of the Lord.

Joshua is a type of Jesus. We who claim Christ as our Lord and Savior are called also to be a type of Joshua, having complete, 100%, total confidence in the power of God, the love of God, and the will of God. This is the foundation of our spirit of courage.

Jesus had the same spirit of courage to be crucified and die a horrible death to save the world from eternal separation from God because of the sinful nature all humans inherited from Adam. This was God's mission to save the future of humanity. Jesus had to relay this dangerous mission to the responsibility to his disciples. Yes, the work God expects from Christ's followers is dangerous. The work is not easy nor without risk Christ's mission for followers requires the spirit of courage.

KEEP MOVING FORWARD

In the beginning of Luke 9, Jesus gives his 12 disciples their mission. He orders them to go out into the world and do what he was doing. He anoints his apprentices with his power and authority to do God's will. They were to use the spirit of courage founded in Holy Spirit power to carry out the mission from God. The spirit of courage is an attitude and a mind-set that depends exclusively on trusting the sovereign God. They had to trust and depend on Jesus for everything he was instructing them to do and be disciplined enough to do them, even when it was scary, risky, and dangerous.

The disciples were given God's power and authority to drive out demons and to heal sick people. Jesus specifically sent them out to preach and to heal. They were commanded not to carry excess baggage or to bring unnecessary provisions and to depend on those people who offered them hospitality. Wherever they preached, they were to have a headquarters in the community and not move from house to house. If people rejected God's message, the disciples were instructed to "shake the dust off your feet when you leave their town." In other words, separate from anything associated with the place that rejected God. If one analyzes the type of training the disciples received from Jesus along with these instructions it is evident that their purpose was to follow after Jesus and do everything that He did.

Since the beginning of time, people have been transferring skills from one generation to another in some form of apprenticeship. Jesus himself was apprenticed to his earthly father Joseph to learn the craft of carpentry. He may have indeed used his father's method of training him, to train his disciples. Jesus taught his disciples to do what he does, say what he says, and believe what he believes. The disciples or pupils of Jesus were supposed to allow the reflection of the light of the Master to shine on the world so that when people looked at them, they recognized Jesus. When they recognized Jesus, they would automatically know His Father. The pupils of our eyes are the expanding and contracting opening in the iris, through which light passes to the retina. In other words, the pupils are designed to regulate the light that enters our eyes. Therefore, through apprenticeship, Jesus' pupils are trained and designed to allow His light to reflect from them and enter into the world.

During apprenticeship there is a progression from total dependence on the master to do the work to complete independence. Once the training is complete, the disciples are to be able to completely take over the work of the master and get the same results. The physical presence of the master is no longer required, they rely solely on what was taught and received during the training. Spiritually, however, the master will always be with his disciple and the disciple will always be with his master.

At the end of Luke chapter 9 verses 57-62, Jesus illustrates the cost of disciples following Him using examples from nature. Jesus is pointing out that saying "I will follow" and actually following are two different things. There is no way to predict where Jesus will lead you so to say "I will follow you wherever you go" is only reliable after careful consideration and acceptance of the potential consequences. There is a cost to following Jesus: pain, suffering, loneliness, separation, rejection, persecution, exposure, and homelessness.

If one were to compare Jesus with birds and foxes; how do you follow after birds and foxes? Their wandering nature makes it difficult to anticipate where they would go. Birds could go high up in the sky and foxes as low as under the earth. One can't even propose to follow them into their homes. Adult birds and foxes don't have homes and their young live in tight places with limited space in the air or under the ground. Unlike young birds that are protected in nests and young foxes in dens; young disciples have no place of refuge. Their only protection comes from God.

Following Jesus demands full attention and commitment to God first. It is interesting that the man in verse 59 said that he needed to bury his father even though his father was obviously still alive and well. If he was sick and dying, the devoted son would not be with Jesus, he would be with his father. Between the time of death and the funeral, an immediate family member of the deceased, such as the son, is called an onen. An onen is obligated to attend to the needs of the deceased and there should be nothing to distract him from these obligations. It is also considered a breach of K'vod Ha-Met or respect for the deceased, to do anything but attend to the deceased. A Jewish funeral is a sacred rite which usually occurs within 24 hours of death. If his father died within the last 7 days, he would have been buried already and his son would be mourning his death (*shivah*).

In some warped way this man believes that if he were to follow Jesus, he would not be able to return home in the future to attend his father's funeral. Otherwise it is a lame excuse not to follow Jesus. I believe the latter. I do not believe Jesus meant that His followers were not going to be able to participate in family gatherings and responsibilities. He just wanted them to make sure that they had their priorities right. The duties to God are higher than duties to family. The duties to God are highest of all.

The man who has to go back and say goodbye to his friends and family is likely never to return. He has doubts and is not ready to completely surrender to God. Emotional support needed for encouragement to follow Jesus comes from being faithful to God. Conferring with the ungodly about godly matters is foolishness. We must keep going forward walking with God.

Walking with God is like plowing. The goal of plowing is to make furrows to plant seeds in anticipation of a harvest. Looking back while plowing will distort the furrows which will affect the seeds and diminish the harvest. Looking back would go against the purpose of plowing in the first place. God says that those who commit themselves to God and then turn back are not capable of being effective in the Kingdom. When we take our eyes off what God has called us to do, we become unable to fulfill God's plan for us.

We must keep our eyes straight ahead. We have to look in the direction that we are going. Putting the hand on the plow means we have decided to plow, we made a choice and we have a mission. If we relax our grip, we are in danger of losing our crop. If we decide to start plowing in one direction we need to continue in that direction. God has given us the most important choice of all. He allows his creation to choose whether or not to follow Him. Once we decide to follow him we must continue our momentum in his divine direction. Looking back is the complete opposite of going forward.

Plowing is a forward moving activity. Following Jesus is also a forward moving activity. Looking back while traveling forward is dangerous behavior that signifies an overwhelming yearning for what was left behind. The person looking back is strongly considering going back in the wrong direction toward evil ways, destruction and even death. Looking back represents following the path of darkness because it is completely opposite from following the light of Jesus and moving forward. Followers of Jesus must focus on Him, His ways, and His words and never deviate from His guiding light. God requires that we be His workers on earth. We are to follow after His agenda and be His apprentices. We are to have His purposes in mind and learn our skills from Him. To this endeavor, God gave us scripture. God is gracious to provide all that we need to do God's work with skill and cunning.

As sons and daughters of God we must seek after God's Truth in all things. In Paul's 2nd letter to Timothy, he is speaks out against teachers of false doctrine. He warns Timothy against the apostasy of Hymenaeus and Philetus. According to 1 Timothy 1:20, they taught that the resurrection of believers had already occurred. This was probably an early form of Gnosticism that emphasized a spiritual resurrection against the Christian belief in a future bodily resurrection. Their false teaching was dangerous like cancer that spreads uncontrollably without permission or boundaries. Chapter 2 verse 15 gives profound instruction to the followers of Jesus: "Do your best to present yourself to God as one approved by him, a worker who has no need to be ashamed, rightly explaining the word of truth."[4]

In response to Gnosticism and other heretical teachings, Paul "exhorts Timothy to strive to handle the word of truth, the gospel that he received from Paul, with correctness. This means in this context that he is to preach and teach it faithfully and exemplify it in his conduct." This scripture begins with the Greek word σπουδάζω (*spoudazō*), which means to strive after with diligence or earnestness. God knows that we are not perfect, but he expects us to always to do our best in our endeavors. The scripture says that we present ourselves as pleasing to God, not man. All our efforts should be toward being acceptable to our Heavenly Father despite the earthly consequences. Inherent in our existence is that God is always looking at us, examining us, and inspecting us. Because of our

---

[4] Schwandt, John ; Collins, C. John: *The ESV English-Greek Reverse Interlinear New Testament*. Logos Research Systems, Inc., 2006; 2006

humanness, we will always come short of God's expectations, but that is no excuse for us not to do our best.

We are to do our best work for the Lord. Our labor is not only physical but spiritual. Those approved by God work for Him and His causes. We must not be counterfeit Christians. The word δόκιμος (*dokimos*), is Greek for accepted, approved and pleasing. In ancient times, dokimos were money changers of integrity who would accept no counterfeit money and would only put genuine full weighted money into circulation.

The same thing is true for Christians, we are to be persons of integrity, who do not accept counterfeit teaching and only preach from the Word of God or λόγος (*logos*). Logos is a Greek word which means doctrine, teaching, and the sayings of God, decree, mandate or order, of the moral precepts given by God. Of course this logos is the Word of Truth and it must be rightly divided by Christians. The phrase rightly divided comes from the Greek word ὀρθοτομέω (*orthotomeō*). This word, which occurs only in this scripture in the New Testament, means "to cut straight," as to cut a straight road or to keep a straight course. The idea could also be that of plowing a straight furrow or of squaring and cutting a stone to fit it in its proper place. In the Old Testament, a similar Hebrew word is used in *Proverbs 3:6* and *11:5* to depict God's provision of a straight path for the righteous. Paul encouraged Timothy to handle the word of truth in a straight way, like a road that goes straight to its goal, without being turned aside by useless debates. In this manner we must diligently teach the truth directly and correctly, always working hard to do what is right.

There are three main themes of the scripture: 1) diligence, 2) work, and 3) teaching. God's servants must live and work to honor Christ. To this end the utmost diligence must be used to please God. This requires a pure life as well as judicious work to present the truth clearly accurately. We are to teach what we already know to be true from the logos and remind our students about the doctrines of truth they have already learned.

2 Timothy 2:15 starts with diligence and flows through consecration and ends in the truth. Diligence and work describe the tremendous effort used by God's servant. Approved and not ashamed describe our sanctification and what God sees in us. The phrase "rightly dividing the word of truth" stands on its own. We must explain the word of truth by dissecting it into its most basic components so that how we teach, how we live, and how we work are an accurate representation of God's truth.

Workman or workwoman for God are expected to work in the spirit of courage. We are to labor for the Lord. God does not expect us to take the easy way out when it comes to God's purpose for our lives. Of course God is merciful and God's mercies are new every morning, but the almighty also provides everything we need to do God's will. God guides us through God's Word and God's Holy Spirit. God also provided for us a rabbi, Jesus Christ.

Jesus Christ, the Son of David, of course is the ultimate rabbi. His existence on this earth changed the entire world for eternity. He was raised in a devotedly Jewish home and received training in Judaism's Oral Law. He was such an expert that He performed rabbinical duties at age 12. His life is our example and our standard. The popular phrase, "what would Jesus do" helps us to remember that the right answers to our questions and problems come from the Son of God. Our rabbi, who sits at the right hand of the Father, loves us beyond understanding, blesses us with overflowing blessings, and knows everything.

But the question is, are we supposed to be someone else's "rabbi" while on this earth? If we are commanded to imitate Christ, does that mean we are supposed to be rabbinical? Yes, Christians should strive to be profoundly wise. We are commanded to work hard and diligently to know the Word of Truth. We are to seek God's truth through His word. The knowledge that is obtained from this endeavor is to be disseminated throughout the world. In other words, God's people are called to spread the knowledge of the Truth globally.

We must always remember that God is omniscient. God knows everything. God knows when we are trying to get away with doing less than what God has commanded us to do. God knows our hearts and we cannot fool God. We must have the courage to focus on impressing God and not people. Christians are to work hard for the purposes of God. It takes purposeful effort and courage to follow God's plan for our lives.

True children of God follow after the Parent like baby ducks follow their mother, in an orderly fashion. We seek guidance as well as approval from God. We are to move about each day in the path the God sets for us. Before God created the foundation of the world and before we were formed in our mother's womb, God had a plan for each person. We are commanded to use the measure of faith we were born with to do God's good will.

There is freedom in living according to God's will. As scholars of His Word, or rabbis, we may know that God imparts wisdom and courage to those who diligently seek after our Creator. Our all-powerful God, who loves us beyond understanding is in control of every aspect of our lives, therefore, we are free. We are free to have the joy and peace that is promised to those who believe in God. How then can we possibly refuse to preach the gospel of Truth to all the world, every day, whether in words or deeds in the spirit of courage?

Reflection Questions

1. Do you obsess over the past?

2. What are your plans for the future?

3. Do you have a mission or calling from God? Are you honoring it and fulfilling it?

ELEVEN

It Takes Courage to go to China

I've always wanted to travel to China. I want to see the whole world that God created and see all of God's people. This is the adventurous side of Tracie. The furthest I've traveled away from the US was to Rome, Italy during my first year of seminary. It was a gift from God. It was also a mission for God. I arrived at seminary already loving the bible, especially the New Testament because that is where I got to know who Jesus is and what Jesus did while on this earth. One way to learn more about the New Testament is to visit Rome. My trip was amazing. It shaped my entire seminary experience. It was a once in a life time opportunity and I knew it from the moment I heard about the trip. I knew in my spirit that I was going to Rome with my seminary. I applied immediately but after several weeks, I did not hear a word from the professor in charge of the trip. Since I already *knew* that I was going to Rome, I had the courage to call the professor and tell him that I was waiting for a response. He said that the trip was full and he didn't recall my application. I insisted that I sent it and he said that he would get back to me. He found my application and he said that he would put me on the waiting list because he was going to ask the sponsors of the trip if two more people could attend. The sponsors said yes and I went to Rome. Not only did I get to go to Rome with my seminary and get two credit hours, I went first class. I had some super saver miles on my credit card and when I called to make my plane reservation, the agent on the phone showed me favor and upgraded me so that I flew to and from Rome in first class. It was wonderful! I was in heaven with Jesus. My trip to Rome was ordained in heaven. It was not only for me but for the people that I preach the Gospel to. The trip was part of my training process. It was very important that I went. But if I did not have the courage to confront the professor that overlooked my application, I never would have went.

Now, five years later I have the opportunity to go to China and I need to have courage again. On several levels this trip to China takes courage. I have to leave my husband and my two kids to go to China. I have to be on a plane for several hours roundtrip cramped in seats not wide enough for my hips or enough legroom for me to stretch out my legs because someone else is making the arrangements. Yes, I'm blessed to go to China on a medical mission for free. The mission is to encourage and teach the medical staff at four hospitals in southwestern China to provide pain relief for pregnant women in labor. At first I wondered why China needs us to travel across the world to teach them about epidurals. They have the technology, they have women doctors, but their culture doesn't see the worth in providing this service to women. This attitude toward women gets my blood boiling, my dander up, my knickers twisted, it gets me mad. So now I'm going to a communist country with an attitude about how their culture is abusive toward women. So a black, Baptist, woman preacher, obstetric anesthesiologist has to chose whether or not to be quiet in China and observe, or speak up and advocate for the Chinese women. By now, after reading this far, you know what I am going to do.

My trip to China is another trip ordained from God. The blessing is not only for me, it is for God's people. As my boss would say, "in actual fact," all of my blessings are for God's people. In other words, God does not bless individuals in isolation, God blesses individuals for communities of individuals. For example, I knew that God called me to go to

Union Theological Seminary to train to be a minister of the Gospel. But, I also knew that I was to be a blessing to the people at Union. I was suppose to bring Jesus Christ to Union in a bold way and I did. I knew that it was my season to be at Union, a once in a life time assignment. In other words, God commanded that I go to seminary in that hotel room in Hampton, Virginia while I attended Hampton University Minister's Conference, June, 2007. God and I struggled and fought. I told God the conditions upon which I would attend seminary and God assured me that I would be blessed, I would not go in debt, I would be able to keep practicing anesthesiology, and most importantly, that my family would remain intact. Reader, I want you know that God is faithful. God is trustworthy. God has the power to back up God's promises. God has no choice but to honor the contracts or covenants he makes with God's people. Hallelujah!

So five years later, I am not struggling with God like I did before going to seminary, but I do have struggles. The biggest struggle on my mind is my body. My body is too large to "fit" in China. I need to lose weight. I imagine Chinese people a very small with small chairs, small space, too small for me to fit. My body is also not fit. I distinctly remember our first day in Rome. We walked around the city for miles going from basilicas, to monuments, to a triumphant arch, to the Coliseum. It was magnificent. I need to be able to do the same amount of walking in China. If the truth be told, God has been telling me for years to lose weight and exercise more and I haven't been obedient. No I don't have a choice. I have to get my body right in order to do what God wants me to do in China.

Sometimes one's credibility is based upon body appearance. There are statistics about how people are treated or viewed based upon their body habitus. In January, 2013, a few days ago, a study from the Rudd Center for Food Policy & Obesity at Yale University came out saying that male jurors were more likely to find overweight women compared with lean women guilty in mock court cases. They also noted that lean men were more likely than overweight men to hand down a guilty verdict to an overweight woman. We still live in a male dominated world. We are getting better, but we have not arrived yet. This news is weighing on my spirit of courage.

I am going to China and I will "fit" in China and the Chinese medical workers will take me seriously because my China mission is ordained by God. I am going to eat less and move more every day until the trip and beyond. This is not the first time God commanded me to do this. About ten years ago I lost approximately one hundred pounds by eating healthy and exercising. I drank a lot of carrot juice, stopped eating carbohydrates and went to the gym at least five times a week. It took a year and I felt great. My goal was to be healthy and fit to be able to run after and play with my very active son who was a toddler at the time. Over the last five years I gained half of it back because I stopped exercising. I went to seminary and stopped exercising, that was a mistake. Now I'm exercising again and I feel great again. I am geared up to go to China with courage.

Lessons Learned and Reflection Questions

1 Are you afraid to do something you know you are suppose to do? Do it anyway.

2 Being obedient to God's plans for your life always results in blessings for you and your children.

3 Is there a place where you think you don't fit?

TWELVE

It Takes Courage To Be In Heaven....Now

I say it all the time, "I'm in heaven." I'm just agreeing with the bible, we are seated in heavenly places with Christ since "before the beginning." We don't know when the beginning was, only the triune God knows. So any concept we humans have of the beginning is not accurate that is why I say "before the beginning" to acknowledge that we don't know when that was. We do know that in the beginning, God created the heavens and the earth. We also know that in the beginning God created mankind. Thus, humankind was created for heaven and earth.

> *But God, who is rich in mercy, out of the great love with which he loved us even when we were dead through our trespasses, made us alive together with Christ*—by grace you have been saved— and raised us up with him and seated us with him in the heavenly places in Christ Jesus*
>
> —EPHESIANS 2:4-6

Humans are body, soul(or mind) and spirit. We were with Christ from "before the beginning" in spirit and God already knew us and chose us. Just in case you don't already know, Jeremiah is an example of any person who calls Christ Savior. Our physical flesh is brought forth on earth and remains on earth. Our souls and bodies do not physically levitate into heaven. We will have a new form in heaven.

> *Now the word of the LORD came to me saying,*
> *5 'Before I formed you in the womb I knew you,*
> *and before you were born I consecrated you;*
> *I appointed you a prophet to the nations.'*
>
> —JEREMIAH 1:4-5

IT TAKES COURAGE TO BE IN HEAVEN....NOW

For it was you who formed my inward parts;
you knit me together in my mother's womb.

—Psalm 139:13

Certainly, the word of God is true. My question to you is do you believe it? I didn't ask you if you feel it, I asked you if you believe it? If you live according to the world view, this message is crazy. If you live according to the word of God, this message is marvelous. God is calling us right now to pick one. There is no in-between. Crazy or marvelous. Another word for crazy is unrealistic. I have been accused of being unrealistic because I choose to focus on the promises of God and not the circumstances of everyday life.

If you are already seated in heaven with Christ, if your spirit is going to heaven when your flesh dies, why not act like you are in heaven now? In fact the conversation I am having with you right now is in heaven. (Philippians 3.20) This is what God calls us to do, seek after the kingdom of God first and everything else comes next. God always has to come first. We have to love God first, worship God first, obey God first, believe God first, ask God first, honor God first, God always comes first. God is always before the beginning.

Advent is the beginning of the celebration of the birth of Christ. The Christmas season focused on the spirit of expectation, anticipation, preparation, and longing. Technically, Christmas is supposed to remind us to expect, anticipate, prepare and long for the second coming of Christ. God is so gracious and patient with us that God gives us chances over and over again to honor God, to accept God, to worship God in spirit and in truth, not only in lip service.

However, my question today is have you already accepted the first coming of Christ?

It makes no sense to teach and preach about the second coming of Christ if people don't accept that Christ was with God "before the beginning" and that he was sent to earth by God to save humanity. Did you accept in your heart that Christ died for your sins? Have you called on Christ to save you? Do you know in your spirit that you have direct contact with God because Jesus died on the Cross for you? When you pray are you sure that God hears every word?

In order to answer these questions it helps to know you are seated in heaven with Christ Jesus. See my friend, how can I tell you to prepare for Christ's second coming if you have not received in your heart Christ's first coming?

Just because you say that you are saved, doesn't make it so. You have to believe and when you believe that Christ died for you there is a supernatural transformation on earth and in heaven. The transforming requires maturing and it never stops. Just like God is forever, so is the transforming and maturing in Christ (Philippians 3). God has called us to heaven in Christ Jesus. This is the blessing.

We must always remember that our blessings and provision comes from almighty God. As we have learned this is the foundation of our courage. This is why our worship services end in a benediction such as:

> *Now to him who is able to keep you from falling, and to make you stand without blemish in the presence of his glory with rejoicing, to the only God our Saviour,*

IT TAKES COURAGE TO BE IN HEAVEN....NOW

through Jesus Christ our Lord, be glory, majesty, power, and authority, before all time and now and forever. Amen.

—JUDE 24,25

Do we believe this awesome benediction? Most people don't. So many people don't believe in the first coming of the Messiah, Jesus Christ. Too many Christians have allowed our faith to become corrupted with the lies of the world. "But you are a chosen race, a royal priesthood, a holy nation, God's own people,* in order that you may proclaim the mighty acts of him who called you out of darkness into his marvelous light." (1 Peter 2:9) Therefore, expect the shining face of God to shine all over your life every day. Shine the spirit of courage all over every aspect of your life, your circumstance and all over the world. This concept is reflected in the attitude of the new light of each day.

When you say "good morning" (*boker tov*) in Hebrew to a Jewish person, the response is "morning of light." (*boker or*)

125

What a way to start the day focused on the light of God. Expect that you will reflect that light back onto the world in your everyday walk and in everything that you do.

As we continue to grow spiritually, we will expect the shining face of God to light our world. This shining face of God is also known as favor or grace. Are you expecting God's favor? If you believe the first coming of Christ, if you believe that Jesus was born of Mary, lived, suffered and died for our sins. If you believe that on the third day, early in the morning, Jesus rose from the dead with all power in his hand then you have favor. Nobody deserves God's favor, it's the gift of God, through our faith in Jesus Christ. All we have to do is receive it.

Receiving Christ is not optional. There is no second coming blessing without receiving the light of the first coming. The light of the first coming is the promise of heaven. How can we claim that we are going to heaven when we die if we don't acknowledge that we are seated in heaven with Christ when our bodies are alive on earth? Whatever is true in heaven is true on earth. My friend be blessed and have the courage it takes to be in heaven.

The LORD bless you and keep you;

> *25 the LORD make his face to shine upon you, and be gracious to you;*
> *26 the LORD lift up his countenance upon you, and give you peace.*
>
> —NUMBERS 6:24-26

Reflection Questions

1   Do you believe the following scriptures?

> *Now the word of the LORD came to me saying,*
> *5 'Before I formed you in the womb I knew you,*
> *and before you were born I consecrated you;*
> *I appointed you a prophet to the nations.'*
>
> —JEREMIAH 1:4-5

> *For it was you who formed my inward parts;*
> *you knit me together in my mother's womb.*
>
> —PSALM 139:13

2   What does heaven mean to you?

THIRTEEN

Courage to be the Voice of Oppressed Women

I use a picture of Sojourner Truth to represent all of the courageous women who fought for women's rights such as Elizabeth Cady Stanton, Mary Church Terrell, Ida B. Wells and many more. They all stood on the truth that women are not sub-human or less than men, especially in the eyes of God. Humankind, including males and females, was created in the image of God. God loves all humans equally, God does not show favoritism. (Acts 10:34) Women are not second class citizens, we are blessed by God according to our faith, not according to men, society or culture. Beware of oppressors, especially those dressed in sheep's clothing. (Matthew 7:15)

Who would ever believe it? God told me to be quiet and listen today in church and I did and God revealed some things to me that I probably had blinders on about before this day. What did I learn:

1. I was called to be a voice for women, especially women that are too scared to speak for themselves when they are being oppressed by men and other figures of power

2. Some pastors may not hear from God in the pulpit

3. Some pastors may have an agenda other than Saving souls

4. Some pastors may lead their church as a dictatorship

5. Some pastors do not value the input and opinions from the people they lead

6. Some pastors focus on getting credit for what they have done in the past to the point that it hinders their future vision of the church

7. Some pastors manipulate the people

8   Some pastors are offensive and hurt the women instead of lead them

9   No pastor is wiser or better than me in the LORD because God gives to me freely

10 I have courage to stand up to oppressors of women

Right when I am about to send my book to the publisher this happens. God wants to make sure that I end this book with the most important message of all. Use the spirit of courage God gave you to speak up and speak out for those who are vulnerable and cannot speak for themselves.

I have been getting in trouble all of my life because of my mouth. I got in trouble with my parents, my grandmother, teachers, professors, physicians, ministers, all who were over me in power and position but were doing wrong. I always wondered why others wouldn't speak out with me. Now I know it doesn't matter why they won't speak out, the issue is that I must because I have the courage and God told me too. God created me this way "before the beginning." My friend have the courage to do what God created you to do by faith. Don't let anybody intimidate you. Don't let anybody manipulate you. Don't be afraid. Let God lead the way through the mess so that God can get all of the glory. You may not be able to see the way but go with God anyway.

About the Author

Rev. Dr. Tracie A. Saunders is an Associate Professor of Anesthesiology and Assistant Professor of Obstetrics, Gynecology, and Reproductive Medicine and has been an Attending Anesthesiologist at SUNY Stony Brook University Medical Center (SBMC) since 1995 after completing her anesthesiology residency at St. Luke's-Roosevelt Medical Center in New York City. She specializes in high risk Obstetric Anesthesiology, is a founding member of the Resource Center for Spirituality and Health Care Education at SBMC, and serves on the SBMC Institutional Ethics Committee. Dr. Saunders earned a Bachelor of Science degree in Mathematics at Spelman College, Atlanta, Georgia in 1985, a medical degree at Boston University School of Medicine in 1990, and a Master of Divinity from Union Theological Seminary of New York City in 2010. She was awarded the Maxwell Fellowship from Auburn Seminary given to those seminary students who show the promise of excellence in future service in parish ministry. The award committee wrote that Dr. Saunders:

> *"cares deeply about the pain and suffering of people and believes that health is a state of complete physical, mental and social well-being, not merely the absence of an infirmity. She brings this empathetic understanding with compassion to her faith community as a teacher and a preacher. She will be a quiet wind of change in any parish setting."*

Dr. Saunders was ordained in the Gospel Ministry at Faith Baptist Church, Coram, New York on December 18, 2010. She has been married to her husband, Eric, Sr. for 27 years and they have been blessed with two children, Amanda and Eric, Jr.

For additional copies of this book please contact the author at tracrahab@msn.com or write to:

Rev. Dr. Tracie Saunders
8 Timber Ridge Court
Coram, NY 11727

www.ingramcontent.com/pod-product-compliance
Lightning Source LLC
Chambersburg PA
CBHW050644160426

43194CB00010B/1795